The Devil Can't Have Me No Matter What...

An INSPIRATIONAL And RELIGIOUS Book

"ALWAYS FOCUS ON GOD"

MARY WILKERSON

The Devil Can't Have Me No Matter What …..
An INSPIRATIONAL and RELIGIOUS Book Always Focus on God
All Rights Reserved.
Copyright © 2020 Mary Wilkerson
v2.0

The opinions expressed in this manuscript are solely the opinions of the author and do not represent the opinions or thoughts of the publisher. The author has represented and warranted full ownership and/or legal right to publish all the materials in this book.

This book may not be reproduced, transmitted, or stored in whole or in part by any means, including graphic, electronic, or mechanical without the express written consent of the publisher except in the case of brief quotations embodied in critical articles and reviews.

ISBN: 978-1-7339235-0-7

Cover and Interior Photos © 2020 Mary & Kerry Wilkerson. All rights reserved - used with permission.

All Scripture quotations are taken from the *New Living Translation Version* of the Bible. Except John 3:16 (*King James Version*)

Excerpt from "The Flat Family Series" and information about Spiritual Life Family Worship Center (Norfolk, VA) is included with permission and courtesy of Pastor William Kent Collins.

PRINTED IN THE UNITED STATES OF AMERICA

THIS BOOK IS DEDICATED AS FOLLOWS

In Loving Memory of
Those That Are In Heaven Waiting

Mom & Dad (Emily & Louie)
My Sister (Barbara)
My Brother (Louis)
My Other Mother (Toni)
My Brother-in-Law (Rich)
Our Pets (Dandy, Xena, Zeus, Baby)

Dedicated To Those
Still Living – I Love You

Kerry
Nina & Apollo
Nette & Dickie
My Sister, Rita and her family
Gracie & Marjorie
All My Wonderful Friends

One of My Favorite Verses

To start this book out right, I wanted to share one of my favorites. This one verse sets the tone for this book. It talks about love, hope, faith, and our everlasting future.

John 3:16 – For God so loved the world that He gave His only begotten son, that whosoever believes in Him will not perish but have everlasting life.

Table of Contents

Thank You I

Introduction. III

A Snapshot of My Life V

Chapter 1: A Little Bit About Mary and
Her Beloved Mom, Emily 1
   Childhood & Love for God. 2
   Emily – Or As I Call Her "Mom" 4
   Life Is A Shock 6
   How To Survive Life 10
   Depression & Loneliness. 13
   Don't Be Afraid – God Cares About Us. 15

Chapter 2: Never Give Up on God. 17
   Kerry - The Love Of My Life 18
   Praying - Constantly 19

    Pray, Believe, & Let Go 21
    Praying + Trust = Enjoy Peace 23
    God Will Not Let Us Fall 25
    One Day At A Time 26
    Don't Take Your Problems Back. 28
    The Beatitudes 30

Chapter 3: All About Jesus 31
    The True Meaning of the Birth of Jesus &
    His Time on Earth 32
    Jesus – The Light Of The World 35
    Faith in God 38
    Our New Spirit In God. 40
    That Old Rugged Cross 44
    Let's Talk About Love 45
    Keep Your Eyes On The Prize 47
    Jesus Is In Control And He Is Coming Back !!. 49

Chapter 4: Life Is Not Easy 51
    Forgive Others. 52
    When God Says No 54
    My Big Plans. 56
    We All Have Gifts. 57
    Focus On God 59
    Our One True Best Friend. 61
    Friends And Extended Family on Earth. 62

Chapter 5: A Grand Future 65
    A New Home 66
    I Hope I Don't Screw It Up 69
    A Work In Progress 72
    All Praise, Glory, & Honor 74
    Our Father Rules The Universe 76

Chapter 6: From Rainbows to Owls 77
    Rainbows 78
    Look At God's Creations and Be Amazed 79
    The Importance & Love of Animals 81
    We Are God's Sheep 82
    Will I See My Pets Again? 83
    Be Wise – Like An Owl 85

Chapter 7: Hide Me Under Your Wings 87
    Some Proverb & Psalm One Liners 88
    Angels Watching Over Us Or "Cool, I Have My Own Angel" 90
    Angels Are Neat – But Jesus Is Better 92
    Endure The Hard Times – Be Blessed 94
    Hide Me Under Your Wings 96

Chapter 8: A Lifetime of Hope 99
    Just Who Is In Control? 100
    Our God Loves Us & He Will Lead Us 102
    The Devil Does Not Win 103

    Let's Talk Death. 105

    The Resurrection of the Dead 108

Chapter 9: Interesting Tidbits in the Bible 111

    God Always Keeps His Promises 112

    The Ark of the Covenant. 114

    We Can Always Rely On God. 117

    We Have Everlasting Hope 119

    Ezekiel – A Fascinating Chapter in the Bible. 120

Chapter 10: The Comforting Chapter 123

    Being Judged. 124

    The Holy Spirit – Our Comforter. 126

    Let's Talk About Spiritual Blessings 129

    The Armor Of God. 131

    Jesus Is Our Everything. 133

Chapter 11: The Return of Jesus 135

    Our New Bodies 136

    The Last Days. 144

    The Rapture 145

    Revelation – A Must Read For Everyone 147

Chapter 12: The Devil Can't Have Me. 159

    The Bible – A Verse A Day 160

    I Hope I Meet You In Heaven. 162

Thank You

I would like to acknowledge and thank the following individuals who have been inspirational and very helpful in putting this book together, providing encouraging words, and helping me understand the dynamics of publishing a book.

Kerry, *my husband – thank you for your support, your love, your belief in God, your patience, and your assistance in every aspect of this book and my life. You instill in me the confidence I have in everything I do. I will never be able to express my love for you and my appreciation for your caring nature, unwavering protection, awesome sense of humor, and your unconditional love that you provide to me. I love you so much.*

William Collins, *my friend and fellow author – a true inspiration and a fantastic Pastor. You are bringing a lot of people to God.*

Emily, *my mom - even though you are no longer physically with me you still have an impact on my life. Your love of me and especially your love of God has kept me on the right path. Until we meet again, I will treasure you forever.*

The Devil Can't Have Me No Matter What, I'll Hit Him In The Head and I'll Kick Him In The Butt......

This was what my mom used to say to me all the time. I *loved* that saying, I still love that saying. When I feel myself getting overwhelmed due to life's circumstances, I focus on God and repeat those words. The devil is working extra hard to get people, but he won't get me. I don't want him to get you either. When I was only 25 years old I thought that by being a good person, loving God and treating people well would be enough to help me get through life's challenges. Boy, was I in for a long eye awakening depressing ride. But my story does have a happy ending.

Before I get too wordy and you lose interest, I need to explain what I went through in my life that brought me to where I am now. I will only use my name (Mary), my husband's name (Kerry), my mother's name (Emily) and those individuals who allowed me to give them credit (and use their names) for their help in my life. Other names will be left out to protect the innocent, or not so innocent.

I feel compelled to write this book. I think God is nudging me to write something a little different than others have written.

I want people to see that through perseverance, faith, trust in God, with a little bit (or a lot) of humor thrown in, you can face any of life's challenges. If I can help even one person become a believer in God and spread the Word, then I will be happy.

My story will be in small doses and will include Bible verses that have helped me. Ones that still help me. I hope they help you too. I wanted something quick and easy to access for those times when you don't feel like reading a lot.

Maybe my story and my mom's story (I will tell hers briefly) will help others, whether you are a caretaker of the sick or elderly (which I have been), or you are a parent, or grandparent, or you are working a full time job and just trying to live your own life, my hope is to help you deal with life a little easier. So, here goes.......

The main focus in this book is and always will be on GOD

A Snapshot of My Life

For 30 years I dealt with depression, sadness, disbelief at being treated so horribly (sometimes by family members) and had my faith shaken so bad that I believed that I turned into a horrible person. I have dealt with sicknesses, job challenges and losses, struggling with self-esteem and felt used all the time. I was a mess. It was a terrible time that I thought would never end.

I was also a caretaker for most of those 30 years. And not just one person, but three. My husband was right by my side and I can honestly say that if it was not for his help, I may not have survived. My husband is a good man and loves God, but sometimes he was a challenge to deal with as well. But I cannot complain – he took on so many roles, more than any other man I have met.

Did we have stressful times? Heck yes. Are we still dealing with stressful situations? Oh yes. But, we got through it and continue to get through life's challenges, thanks to the Grace of God. And so can you. Just don't give up on God. My mother told me that, and she was right. I listened and in time I understood. I wished I had known this earlier in life. But no regrets, I cannot change the past. God allows things to happen in our lives for reasons we cannot understand. But at the right time, and if you trust Him, He will make things clear to you.

I watched my mother deal with tough situations with calm and patience and she never lost her faith in God. She never yelled at Him (I did), she never lost her temper with others (boy did I). She always hung to this saying – "The Devil Can't Have Me….".

I always wished I could be more like my mom. Up until the time she passed away, she always told me to "Never give up on God" and that she would find a way to drag me with her into Heaven, even if she had to come down and snatch me herself.

We were very close. And you know what, we still are. I can feel her. After she passed away in 2018, I felt like I became part of her somehow. Something happened to me. It is like I took on her personality. Suddenly I wanted to learn everything I could about God. I know how crazy that sounds and I cannot explain it well.

A peace came over me and I know she is in Heaven with my dad, my sister, my brother, other family members, and our treasured pets throughout the years. This earthly life is a short trip, the destination is where we all need to strive to be.

You will find snippets from my experiences mixed with Bible verses.

CHAPTER 1
A Little Bit About Mary and Her Beloved Mom, Emily

Mom

Childhood & Love for God

My childhood was wonderful. My mom was my best friend and I absolutely adored her. I had a few childhood friends, but none of them compared to mom. She made me laugh – we have the same sense of humor. She made me smile – we had made up names (our own language that only she and I knew) for mean people and difficult situations. She gave me my love of reading and writing. I love to write scripts (for movies and TV). I have been writing stories and scripts since I was small (I just didn't know I was doing it). She gave me my love for words. For example, we loved the word "suddenly". It is an exciting word. Maybe not to some people, but to us it was like stepping into another world. But what she gave me the most, was my love for God.

My dad was great my whole life. He was my bowling and golf buddy and I loved him. My sisters were quite a few years older and both married with children, so I never really got to bond with them too much. I loved them always. But nobody could touch the bond with my mom. Mom had me late in life and I was her baby, up until the day she passed away.

My mom and I loved Revelation in the Bible. We longed to be taken up in the rapture together. I grew up in Massachusetts and one time in a department store, I had gone in search of something (I don't remember what), but I do remember hearing my mom frantically calling for me. When I found her she was relieved. She was afraid that I had gone up in the rapture without her. We had a good laugh, but we always remembered that. To this day, I am looking forward to the rapture. I hope that everyone reads Revelation. Oh what hope it gives to us.

My mom's name was Emily. She was the sweetest person you would ever want to meet. Even when she lost her eyesight she had me type up inspirational papers about God so she and my dad could give them out to their friends and strangers they met (even at the grocery store). Mom was a writer too. She used to make me these loving, funny notes that she put in my lunch (even when I was in my 20's and going to work). I have kept them all. I treasure them as I treasured her. Mom used to call herself "Lonesome Tex" – that is the name she used when she wrote. She wrote poems (I still have those) and she and I even created our own stories together.

Emily – Or As I Call Her "Mom"

My mother was born in February (the month of love) and that was perfect. She was true love and showed that love to everyone. Any chance she got she would talk about God. Her life was not easy. As the first born in her family and as the one expected to do everything, she did so without complaint. Her father died when she was young and she was raised by a step-father who did not like her much. She described her own mother as being "like a child".

Although she was born in the United States, her parents were not. Mom only spoke Italian at least until she got into school. My mom not only taught herself, her parents and her sisters how to speak English, the teachers asked her to teach other children in school who could not speak English. My mom took on this task without complaint. She loved to read and write, so this was special to her to help others.

She got married in her twenties and had three children. I came along much later. It was not an easy marriage, but my parents stayed together – for over 60 years. My parents lost their first and only son from cancer when he was young. I never met him, but from what I was told he was a wonderful person. I was told he loved God and never gave up, despite what he was going through.

When I came along mom was always there for me. I remember her singing songs about God when I was very small. Besides her phenomenal sense of humor, that she passed along to me, she always made sure that God played a role in my life. I used to help wash dishes and recite the Lord's Prayer. She was very instrumental in keeping me on the right path my entire life.

I never did anything that I thought could get God mad at me. I did not want to take the chance. I remember telling one priest that my only goal was to make it to heaven.

Later on in life, I went through some terrible times and I did not always ask for advice or let my mom know what was going on. I really did not want her to think bad of me or even be stressed by what I was experiencing. But, she knew. And she never ever gave up on me. In fact, she told me that she was going to make sure I got up there so I could be in Heaven with her and Jesus.

I wish everyone could have known her. Anyone that crossed her path loved her. I loved her very much and always will. Until we meet again, she is still with me.

Life Is A Shock

In my twenties, I was so naïve. I just wanted to write my stories and live in the world I created for my characters. I wanted to live a good life and make my parents and God proud of me. I liked being a good girl. I had no clue what I was doing as far as living in the real world.

When I met my husband, I knew he was the one for me. My family was not so sure, especially my mom. But, Kerry proved himself to my parents and they both came to love him.

It was not an easy dating relationship and I know I hurt a lot of people during those years. I had no idea what I was doing; I trusted when I should have questioned; I was so set on being with Kerry that nothing else mattered. I made mistakes and I cannot even begin to apologize to those I hurt. Oh, they hurt me too. I literally had nobody that I could talk to. I am afraid I hurt my mom the most. I loved her so much, but she had a hard time letting me go and letting me make mistakes. She was my mom and best friend and so protective. I hope she knows how much I appreciated her and my dad.

At the time, I felt like I went through hell on earth. My home life was challenging and stressful, work was difficult (isn't it always?). I lost weight, I could not eat, I got depressed, and I lost my way. I did not trust people – anyone. I thought that I had lost God.

I wish I could say that this only lasted a few years, but in reality, it lasted for more years than I want to consider. I was not easy to live with.

I kept to myself, I distanced myself, I talked to nobody, I trusted no-one, I argued, I yelled, I cried, I was physically sick (migraines, etc.), I yelled at God, I went into my own world. I wish I could do those years over with more patience and understanding. But while I was going through them I did not know how to stop myself from feeling depressed and lonely. It was overwhelming.

I had so much stress that I was about to explode. Dealing with sicknesses, doing everything for others and barely anything for myself, going through rough times at work, misunderstandings about what was going on in life, not understanding where the heck God was in all of this – really took a toll on me.

Then we became caretakers. My husband and I literally went from caring for his mother (who got sick), to becoming full time caretakers for my parents as they got older (both my mom and dad). My parents lived with us until the day they died. I had never been away from my parents. It was difficult living a life with my parents watching our mistakes – the uncertainty of situations, the disagreements, trying to learn to be together, working a full time stressful job – all with no privacy. My husband and I could never have alone time. There was nowhere in the house that was private. It was the way we had to live. Although I would not change having them with us, it was difficult.

I did not handle all of this very well. My emotions and patience were shot. I had no idea what I was doing most of the time, I reacted terribly to even the smallest situation. I tried praying but I never let go of my problems so God could act. I believed I was being targeted by the devil.

Throw in losing some very treasured pets during these years and I am shocked I came through it okay. Like my mom I am an animal lover. My husband is an animal lover too. We have had a few pets and lost them through the years. Losing our sweet bunny (Xena) was the worst experience of loss I had ever felt. She was only six years old and passed away from breast cancer – a rarity for a female bunny that was fixed.

My pets became my best friends and confidants so it was really hard on me to lose her. We did everything we could, but we could not save her. I was devastated for years. We got another bunny, his name is Apollo and he is still with us. But I still miss that sweet bunny.

Right now we have a much loved dog. Her name is Nina. She is Kerry's first dog and she is his dog. She loves him so much. I am the lady that gives her treats. She loves me too, but she is Kerry's dog. I love that he is experiencing a dog. She gives us so much love. A true gift from God.

Even though these years were difficult and I felt like I had lost it all, I came through it okay. And….I didn't lose anything. I never stopped loving God. I may have strayed and thought I lost Him, but God never gave up on me. He patiently waited for me to return to Him.

So, despite whatever trials and tribulations you are going through right now, no matter how desperate your situation may feel to you, it is never too late to trust God.

God loves us so much. This is not our world. So, hang in there. Do not ever give up on God.

If you are desperate, desolate, feel like there is nothing left… stop right there and read on. God's Grace can help us in any situation. There is nothing God cannot do – we just have to trust and believe. No matter the outcome – God is still there for you.

I am not a celebrity, nor am I a religious teacher, I am just an ordinary person who wants to make it to heaven and wants to help others get there as well.

So, I sincerely hope this helps even one person come to God.

How To Survive Life

Mom was right. Never give up on God. Mom told me, actually sung to me, to "pray and believe and invisible hands will help me". She wasn't talking about a ghost. She was talking about God. Mom told me that life is hard, but we are only passing through this life of trials. Our true home, with God, awaits us and we want to make it there.

Look to the future, do not give up!

Psalm 27:1-4 – The Lord is my light and my salvation, so why should I be afraid? The Lord is my fortress protecting me from danger, so why should I tremble?

When evil people come to devour me, when my enemies and foes attack me, they will stumble and fall. Though a mighty army surrounds me, my heart will not be afraid. Even if I am attacked, I will remain confident.

The one thing I ask of the Lord – the thing I seek most – is to live in the house of the Lord all the days of my life, delighting in the Lord's perfections and meditating in his Temple.

Remember, Jesus died for us. He will return for us. This is just a place. Just somewhere that we are visiting. We can do this – we just have to hold on, be patient and wait. Turn to God while you can, before it is too late.

Hebrews 9:27-28 – And just as each person is destined to die once and after that comes judgement.

So, also Christ was offered once for all time as a sacrifice to take away the sins of many people. He will come again, not to deal with our sins, but to bring salvation to all who are eagerly waiting for him.

We have hope…..

John 17:24 – Father, I want these whom you have given me to be with me where I am. Then they can see all the glory you gave me because you loved me even before the world began!

Psalm 84:10-12 – A single day in your courts is better than a thousand anywhere else! I would rather be a gatekeeper in the house of my God than live the good life in the homes of the wicked.

For the Lord God is our sun and our shield. He gives us grace and glory. The Lord will withhold no good thing from those who do what is right.

O Lord of Heaven's Armies, what joy for those who trust in you.

Psalm 86:1-2 –Bend down, O Lord, and hear my prayer; answer me, for I need your help. Protect me, for I am devoted to you. Save me, for I serve you and trust you. You are my God.

Psalm 86:5 – O Lord, you are so good, so ready to forgive, so full of unfailing love for all who ask for your help.

Depression & Loneliness

I learned the hard way that you cannot fight depression alone. Because I was so depressed I became very lonely. I did not trust people and I felt like my faith in God was smaller than a mustard seed. I felt like God abandoned me. Of course He didn't, He was just waiting for me to come to Him.

Circumstances, health issues, stress, just living, can suck the life right out of you. But, we have someone who we can turn to that will NEVER let us down.

Psalm 34:6 – In my depression I prayed and the Lord listened; he saved me from all my troubles.

Psalm 34:17-19 – The Lord hears his people when they call to him for help. He rescues them from all their troubles. The Lord is close to the brokenhearted; he rescues those whose spirits are crushed. The righteous person faces many troubles; but the Lord comes to the rescue each time.

We have someone that really loves us – God. Don't be sad when situations look so bleak we can hardly stand it – stop and focus on the one that is always there for us – no matter what – God. It took me years to learn this lesson. I experienced depression and loneliness, but God never gave up on me. He won't give up on you either.

Psalm 42:5 – Why am I discouraged? Why is my heart so sad? I will put my hope in God. I will praise him again – my Savior and my God.

Don't let this world get you down, it's not our world.

Ecclesiastes 3:11 – Yet God has made everything beautiful for its own time. He has planted eternity in the human heart, but even so, people cannot see the whole scope of God's work from beginning to end.

Psalm 86:11-13 – Teach me your ways, O Lord, that I may live according to your truth! Grant me purity of heart, so that I may honor you.

With all my heart I will praise you, O Lord my God. I will give glory to your name forever, for your love for me is very great. You have rescued me from the depths of death.

Psalm 90:1-2 – Lord, through all the generations you have been our home!

Before the mountains were born, before you gave birth to the earth and the world, from beginning to end, you are God.

2 Peter 3:13 – But we are looking forward to the new heavens and new earth he has promised, a world filled with God's righteousness.

Don't Be Afraid – God Cares About Us

I have fears – spiders, snakes, and the worst being my fear of fire. But when I was going through the depression and anxiety, my real fear was that God left me. I was afraid to tell anyone my problems. The only one I felt I could trust was my mom. But my dad never really let her have alone time with me, so I could not talk to her either.

It was a very isolated time in my life. Those times that I did talk to my mom she always told me to not be afraid, trust God, and keep praying.

My mom was very wise. I still get afraid at times, but my fears diminish since I know that God has my back.

Psalm 56:3-4 – But when I am afraid, I will put my trust in you. I praise God for what he has promised. I trust God, so why should I be afraid? What can mere mortals do to me?

Psalm 56:8 – You keep track of all my sorrows. You have collected all my tears in your bottle. You have recorded each one in your book.

Psalm 56:13 – For you have rescued me from death; you have kept my feet from slipping. So now I can walk in your presence, O God, in your life giving light.

Matthew 7:7-8 –Keep on asking and you receive what you ask for. Keep on seeking and you find. Keep on knocking and the door will be opened to you. For everyone who asks, receives. *Everyone who seeks, finds. And to everyone who knocks, the door will be opened.*

Psalm 91:1-2 – Those who live in the shelter of the Most High will find rest in the shadow of the Almighty. This I declare about the Lord; for he is my God, and I trust Him.

Psalm 92:4-5 – You thrill me, Lord, with all you have done for me! I sing for joy because of what you have done. O Lord, what great works you do! And how deep are your thoughts.

Psalm 94:22 – But the Lord is my fortress; my God is the mighty rock where I hide.

1 Peter 5:7 – Give all your worries and cares to God, for he cares about you.

Matthew 6:30 – And if God cares so wonderfully for wildflowers that are here today and thrown into the fire tomorrow, he will certainly care for you. Why do you have so little faith?

CHAPTER 2
Never Give Up on God

Mary and Kerry

Kerry - The Love Of My Life

Have you ever met someone and just knew that they were the one for you? Someone sent by God. Ever since I was small I had prayed to meet that one person, I only wanted to date once and marry once. I asked God to send me a man who loved God, was close to his parents, would have the same sense of humor as me, and would love me. God sent me Kerry – what a blessing and an answer to my prayers. Although we had some rough patches (who doesn't?), we are so compatible. He can look at me and I know what he is thinking – we are in tune. He was so good to my parents. Kerry was the best caretaker. He did everything for his mother. He loves me and continually goes above and beyond to make me happy. He is a loyal and trustworthy friend to anyone who is lucky enough to become his friend.

When I am sad, he wants to make me happy. When I am mad, he wants to hug me. He waited patiently through my crazy years. He shows me love, compassion, patience, and is my rock on this earth. Kerry makes me feel loved, secured and treasured. Thank God for Kerry.

Kerry did not have an easy life. Yet, he never gave up on God. He is such a good person. Even though most of our lives we were caretakers and we never got the chance to have children, our pets fill that space. Our love of animals, our sense of humor, our respect for each other, everything about us fits so well that I know God put us together. Thank you God !!!

Ephesians 5:33 – So again I say, each man must love his wife as he loves himself and the wife must respect her husband.

Praying - Constantly

When I was growing up I always clung to what was told to me – "pray and it will be given to you". Wow, was I disappointed. That really tripped me up. I prayed for everything and thought my life would be a charm. When nothing got answered, I got frustrated and then I got angry. I doubted myself – was I praying right? Was I a good person? Did I cause this situation that I am going through?

What I now realize is that praying is really a conversation with God. God already has a plan for our lives. He knows what is going to happen – good or bad. We just have to pray and trust and wait for His answer. Good or bad to us, God knows what He is doing. He is in control. We may not understand it or even like it, but we have to trust that God knows what is best for us – even if we don't see it at the time.

We should never let bad circumstances affect our relationship with God. Mom told me not to let circumstances control me, but to trust God with them. Another thing my mom said was to pray always, never stop praying or believing. She told me that God will answer me. I just needed to be patient and trust Him.

Psalm 27:8 – My heart has heard you say, Come and talk with me. And my heart responds, Lord, I am coming.

I Thessalonians 5:17 - Never stop praying.

Romans 12:12 – Rejoice in our confident hope. Be patient in trouble and keep on praying.

Hebrews 13:15 – Therefore, let us offer through Jesus a continual sacrifice of praise to God, proclaiming our allegiance to his name.

Psalm 86:1-7 –Bend down, O Lord and hear my prayer; answer me, for I need your help. Protect me, for I am devoted to you. Save me, for I serve you and trust you. You are my God.

Be merciful to me, O Lord, for I am calling on you constantly. Give me happiness, O Lord, for I give myself to you. O Lord, you are so good, so ready to forgive, so full of unfailing love for all who ask for your help.

Listen closely to my prayer, O Lord; hear my urgent cry. I will call to you whenever I am in trouble, and you will answer me.

Pray, Believe, & Let Go

I still struggle with this daily. This is so much easier to say than to do. But, I am trying and I do see a difference in my life.

Every morning I ask God to put a special protective shield around Kerry, Apollo, Nina, and myself. I ask for protection from evil death, evil sicknesses, evil people, evil situations and evil beings. This is a spirit filled world and not all the spirits are nice.

So, I pray and I ask God to help me with my fears, my requests, protection on our jobs, that we can pay our bills, that we grow old together, whatever else I need help with. Then I hand them over to God.

I try to live just for today. I don't look back at the past (unless I want to depress myself – which I don't); I don't look at my mistakes (which I still make) because Jesus died on the cross for our sins (He forgave me, why should I continue to not forgive me). I confess my sins and rely on God's Grace for forgiveness. I don't look at tomorrow (we are not promised even a second). This relieves a lot of stress.

Revelation 3:20 – Look! I stand at the door and knock. If you hear my voice and open the door, I will come in, and we will share a meal together as friends.

1 Peter 5:7 – Give all your worries and cares to God, for he cares about you.

Patience has not always been my strong point, but I am trying. The end result – living with God forever – is worth being patient.

Psalm 27:14 – Wait patiently for the Lord. Be brave and courageous. Yes, wait patiently for the Lord.

Psalm 95:1-7 – Come, let us sing to the Lord! Let us shout joyfully to the Rock of our salvation. Let us come to him with thanksgiving. Let us sing psalms of praise to him.

For the Lord is a great God, a great King above all gods. He holds in his hands the depths of the earth and the mightiest mountains. The sea belongs to him, for he made it. His hands formed the dry land, too.

Come, let us worship and bow down. Let us kneel before the Lord our maker, for he is our God.

We are the people he watches over, the flock under his care.

Romans 12:12 – Rejoice in our confident hope. Be patient in trouble, and keep on praying.

2 Thessalonians 1:11 – So we keep on praying for you, asking our God to enable you to live a life worthy of his call. May he give you the power to accomplish all the good things your faith prompts you to do.

Praying + Trust = Enjoy Peace

Trust – a big word for me. I struggled with trust in the past. I still struggle with trust in human beings. But I am trusting God. People will disappoint you. God will not. That does not mean that I do not have fears and anxieties or feel guilty, but I stop myself and remember to give these struggles to God (by praying and trusting), a peace comes over me. A peace only God can give me (and you).

Just be honest with your prayer. Praying will not change the world or even change evil people (or circumstances), but it will change you. Prayer gives you the peace to face the challenges of the day.

When you experience a challenge (anger, mean or stupid people or situations), take a deep breath and give it to God. Try it, it really works!

Psalm 25:1-5 – O Lord, I give my life to you. I trust in you, my God. Do not let me be disgraced, or let my enemies rejoice in my defeat. No one who trusts in you will ever be disgraced, but disgrace comes to those who try to deceive others. Show me the right path, O Lord, point out the road for me to follow. Lead me by your truth and teach me, for you are the God who saves me. All day long I put my hope in you.

Psalm 37:5 – Commit everything you do to the Lord. Trust him and he will help you.

Psalm 37:7 – Be still in the presence of the Lord and wait patiently for him to act. Don't worry about evil people who prosper or fret about their wicked schemes.

God Will Not Let Us Fall

I have a great imagination and have been blessed with the ability to "see" things in my mind. A sentence to some is a movie in my mind. Take Psalm 37:23-24. Some people will just read these sentences. I picture myself walking with God while he holds my hand. I see God stopping me from tripping on a crack in the sidewalk. I see God holding me while I cried over anything that was bothering me. I got this great gift of writing and imagination from God. But my mom also made me aware of it. She had the same blessing. Thank you God.

So, although we may stumble through life, God will not allow us to fall. What an amazing God.

Psalm 37:23-24 – The Lord directs the steps of the godly. He delights in every detail of their lives. Though they stumble, they will never fall, for the Lord holds them by the hand.

Nahum 1:7 – The Lord is good, a strong refuge when trouble comes. He is close to those who trust in him.

Don't worry about tomorrow. You have enough on your plate for today.

Matthew 6:34 – Don't worry about tomorrow, for tomorrow will bring its own worries. Today's trouble is enough for today.

One Day At A Time

I used to worry about everything. Even things that I could not control. Oh wait, I cannot control anything, just the way that I react to whatever happens. My mom used to sing to me to take it "one day at a time, sweet Jesus". I used to roll my eyes. I mean, come on, it seems like all day long I am dealing with idiots at work (no names, just a general statement – we all have them at work); stress at home, bills, headaches, the list goes on and on. One day at a time seemed impossible. But then I really thought about what mom said – take it one day at a time and trust God.

Again, mom was right. Do you see a pattern here? Listen to moms…pray….and trust God.

I am finally taking her advice. My new mantra is: I will not look back (at things I cannot change), I will not look forward (at things I cannot control), I will only look at today (moment by moment). I will give my problems, concerns, anxieties, challenges and fears to God. I will trust God and not worry about anything that occurs. I know that God is in control.

Philippians 4:6-7 – Don't worry about anything; instead, pray about everything. Tell God what you need, and thank him for all he has done. Then you will experience God's peace, which exceeds anything we can understand. His peace will guard your hearts and minds as you live in Christ Jesus.

Our time on this earth is very short. Remember, we are just passing through. So we need to always keep our eyes on God. We never want to focus so much on earthly things (which don't even really belong to us), that we miss the opportunity to live with God forever.

Psalm 39:4-7 – Lord, remind me how brief my time on earth will be. Remind me that my days are numbered – how fleeting my life is.

You have made my life no longer than the width of my hand. My entire lifetime is just a moment to you at best, each of us is but a breath.

We are merely moving shadows, all our busy rushing ends in nothing. We heap up wealth, not knowing who will spend it. And so, Lord, where do I put my hope? My only hope is in you.

Isaiah 26:4 – Trust in the Lord always, for the Lord God is the eternal Rock.

John 12:44 – Jesus shouted to the crowds, If you trust me, you are trusting not only me, but also God who sent me.

Don't Take Your Problems Back

Okay, so you give your problems to God in prayer. And then what do we do? We take it back. Oh we say we are waiting for God to answer it and all the while we are working non-stop to fix it ourselves. We humans can be so stubborn. I can only speak for myself when I say that I have a tendency to want to fix things. Patience has never been my strong suit. But it is never too late to change. Pray, trust and believe in God.

I have to constantly resist the urge to take back my problem. I want answers now. I hate waiting. But, I have to trust. God is in control. Evil seems to win, but it doesn't. This is not our world. This world is full of evil, sickness, depression, desperation, all due to the sins of man. We are only visiting. We will talk more on this later – very exciting !! But for now, do not take your problems back. Let God take care of them. We are talking about a God that created everything and He loves us unconditionally. There is nothing impossible with God.

Again I will speak for myself in hopes of helping others. Although I cannot see His purpose or His plan for my life, I know that God is in firm control of the universe and my life. So, I will trust Him with my life. God can handle any problem I give Him. I do not need to take any problems back.

James 1:12 – God blesses those who patiently endure testing and temptation. Afterward they will receive the crown of life that God has promised to those who love him.

Trust God and let your "light" shine so you can bring others to Jesus. Glorify God in all you do – people watch what we do. Showing you trust God when dealing with problems is an inspiration to others. They will want what you have – God.

Ephesians 2:8-10 – God saved you by his grace when you believed. And you can't take credit for this; it is a gift from God. Salvation is not a reward for the good things we have done, so none of us can boast about it. For we are God's masterpiece. He has created us anew in Christ Jesus, so we can do the good things he planned for us long ago.

Psalm 100:1-5 – Shout with joy to the Lord, all the earth! Worship the Lord with gladness. Come before him, singing with joy.

Acknowledge that the Lord is God! He made us, and we are his. We are his people, the sheep of his pasture.

Enter his gates with thanksgiving; go into his courts with praise. Give thanks to him and praise his name.

For the Lord is good. His unfailing love continues forever, and his faithfulness continues to each generation.

The Beatitudes

So what does the word Beatitude mean? According to the dictionary it is a noun referring to a state of great joy. The Latin word beatus means both happy and blessed.

The Beatitudes in the Bible are a series of eight blessings.

Read these and see what blessings you may have in store.

Matthew 5:3-10

God blesses those who are poor and realize their need for him, for the Kingdom of Heaven is theirs.

God blesses those who mourn, for they will be comforted.

God blesses those who are humble, for they will inherit the whole earth.

God blesses those who hunger and thirst for justice, for they will be satisfied.

God blesses those who are merciful, for they will be shown mercy.

God blesses those whose hearts are pure, for they will see God.

God blesses those who work for peace, for they will be called the children of God.

God blesses those who are persecuted for doing right, for the Kingdom of Heaven is theirs.

CHAPTER 3
All About Jesus

Our Sweet Xena

The True Meaning of the Birth of Jesus & His Time on Earth

Christmas is such a wonderful time of the year. People are kind to one another, there are hugs and parties and gifts. But amongst the festivities we sometimes lose sight of the true meaning of the birth of Christ. There is so much focus on Santa, elves, snowmen and reindeer, that the baby in the manger can get lost in the shuffle.

Have no fear, here is a reminder of what Jesus did for you and me.

Luke 2:8-14 – That night there were shepherds staying in the fields nearby, guarding their flocks of sheep. Suddenly, an angel of the Lord appeared among them, and the radiance of the Lord's glory surrounded them. They were terrified. But the angel reassured them – Don't be afraid, he said. I bring you good news that will bring great joy to all people. The Savior – yes, the Messiah, the Lord – has been born today in Bethlehem, the city of David.

And you will recognize him by this sign – you will find a baby wrapped snugly in strips of cloth, lying in a manger. Suddenly the angel was joined by a vast host of others – the armies of heaven – praising God and saying – Glory to God in highest heaven, and peace on earth to those with whom God is pleased.

On a daily basis we are tempted by the devil and his evil minions. Jesus loves us so much that He went through a lot of the trials and tribulations we go through. He even got tempted by the devil.

Luke 4:4-12 – Then Jesus, full of the Holy Spirit, returned from the Jordan River. He was led by the Spirit in the wilderness, where he was tempted by the devil for forty days. Jesus ate nothing all that time and became very hungry. Then the devil said to him, if you are the Son of God, tell this stone to become a loaf of bread.

But Jesus told him – No, the Scriptures say people do not live by bread alone.

Then the devil took him up and revealed to him all the kingdoms of the world in a moment of time. I will give you the glory of the kingdoms and authority over them, the devil said, because they are mine to give to anyone I please. I will give it all to you if you will worship me.

Jesus replied, the Scriptures say you must worship the Lord your God and serve only him.

Then the devil took him to Jerusalem, to the highest point of the Temple and said, if you are the Son of God, jump off. For the Scriptures say – he will order his angels to protect and guard you. And they will hold you up with their hands so you won't even hurt your foot on a stone.

Jesus responded – the Scriptures also say, you must not test the Lord your God.

Jesus went through a lot when He was earthbound, but He did it all to save us. He died on the cross for our sins, so that we may be able to be with Him forever. He rose from the dead to do away with death. All praise, glory and honor to the Father, Son, and Holy Spirit.

Luke 24:44-49 – Then he said, when I was with you before, I told you that everything written about me in the law of Moses and the prophets and in the Psalms must be fulfilled.

Then he opened their minds to understand the Scriptures. And he said, yes it was written long ago that the Messiah would suffer and die and rise from the dead on the third day.

It was also written that this message would be proclaimed in the authority of his name to all the nations, beginning in Jerusalem – there is forgiveness of sins for all who repent. You are witnesses of all these things.

And now I will send the Holy Spirit, just as my Father promised. But stay here in the city until the Holy Spirit comes and fills you with power from heaven.

Jesus – The Light Of The World

I love lighthouses. They are a beacon of hope to those at sea. There is just something about these majestic structures.

Jesus is the real lighthouse of the world. He is our beacon of hope in the rough seas of life. He is truly majestic. Jesus is our Eternal Word and Eternal Hope.

John 1:1-5 – In the beginning the Word already existed. The Word was with God and the Word was God. He existed in the beginning with God. God created everything through him, and nothing was created except through him. The Word gave life to everything that was created, and his life brought light to everyone. The light shines in the darkness and the darkness can never extinguish it.

John 8:12 – Jesus spoke to the people once more and said, I am the light of the world. If you follow me, you won't have to walk in darkness, because you will have the light that leads to life.

Jesus is the Son of God and believing in Him gives us eternal life.

John 5:19-30 – So Jesus explained, I tell you the truth, the Son can do nothing by himself. He does only what he sees the Father doing. Whatever the Father does, the Son also does.

For the Father loves the Son and shows him everything he is doing. In fact, the Father will show him how to do even greater works than healing this man. Then you will truly be astonished.

For just as the Father gives life to those he raises from the dead, so the Son gives life to anyone he wants. In addition, the Father judges no one. Instead, he has given the Son absolute authority to judge, so that everyone will honor the Son, just as they honor the Father. Anyone who does not honor the Son is certainly not honoring the Father who sent him.

I tell you the truth, those who listen to my message and believe in God who sent me have eternal life. They will never be condemned for their sins, but they have already passed from death into life.

And I assure you that the time is coming, indeed it's here now, when the dead will hear my voice—the voice of the Son of God. And those who listen will live. The Father has life in himself, and he has granted that same life-giving power to his Son. And he has given him authority to judge everyone because he is the Son of Man.

Don't be so surprised! Indeed, the time is coming when all the dead in their graves will hear the voice of God's Son, and they will rise again. Those who have done good will rise to experience eternal life, and those who have continued in evil will rise to experience judgment.

I can do nothing on my own. I judge as God tells me. Therefore, my judgment is just, because I carry out the will of the one who sent me, not my own will.

Jesus is our very own Light of The World. Who needs a lighthouse when we have Jesus.

Matthew 5:14 – You are the light of the world – like a city on a hilltop that cannot be hidden.

John 8:12 – Jesus spoke to the people once more and said, I Am the light of the world. If you follow me, you won't have to walk in darkness, because you will have the light that leads to life.

2 Samuel 22:29 – O Lord, you are my lamp. The Lord lights up my darkness.

1 John 1:7 – But if we are living in the light, as God is in the light, then we have fellowship with each other, and the blood of Jesus, his Son, cleans us from all sin.

2 Corinthians 4:6 – For God who said, Let there be light in the darkness, has made this light shine in our hearts so we could know the glory of God that is seen in the face of Jesus Christ.

Faith in God

What does the word faith mean? Faith is a complete trust or confidence in someone or something; a strong belief in God.

According to the Bible, faith in God brings joy for us. Let us see how that works.

Romans 5:5-11 –

Therefore, since we have been made right in God's sight by faith, we have peace with God because of what Jesus Christ our Lord has done for us. Because of our faith, Christ has brought us into this place of undeserved privilege where we now stand, and we confidently and joyfully look forward to sharing God's glory.

We can rejoice, too, when we run into problems and trials, for we know that they help us develop endurance. And endurance develops strength of character, and character strengthens our confident hope of salvation. And this hope will not lead to disappointment. For we know how dearly God loves us, because he has given us the Holy Spirit to fill our hearts with his love.

When we were utterly helpless, Christ came at just the right time and died for us sinners. Now, most people would not be willing to die for an upright person, though someone might perhaps be willing to die for a person who is especially good. But God showed his great love for us by sending Christ to die for us while we were still sinners.

And since we have been made right in God's sight by the blood of Christ, he will certainly save us from God's condemnation. For since our friendship with God was restored by the death of his Son while we were still his enemies, we will certainly be saved through the life of his Son. So now we can rejoice in our wonderful new relationship with God because our Lord Jesus Christ has made us friends of God.

Psalm 57:10-11 – For your unfailing love is as high as the heavens. Your faithfulness reaches to the clouds.

Psalm 103:19-22 – The Lord has made the heavens his throne; from there he rules over everything.

Praise the Lord, you angels, you mighty ones who carry out his plans, listening for each of his commands.

Yes, praise the Lord, you armies of angels who serve him and do his will. Praise the Lord, everything he has created, everything in all his kingdom. Let all that I am praise the Lord.

Deuteronomy 32:4 – He is the Rock; his deeds are perfect. Everything he does is just and fair. He is a faithful God who does no wrong; how just and upright he is!

Our New Spirit In God

Because Jesus died for our sins, and because we believe and confess our sins, and with the help of the Holy Spirit, we have a new spirit in God.

The best news is that nothing can separate us from God's love. Isn't that amazing??

Romans 8 – in its entirety

<u>*Life in the Spirit*</u>

So now there is no condemnation for those who belong to Christ Jesus. And because you belong to him, the power of the life-giving Spirit has freed you from the power of sin that leads to death. The law of Moses was unable to save us because of the weakness of our sinful nature. So God did what the law could not do. He sent his own Son in a body like the bodies we sinners have. And in that body God declared an end to sin's control over us by giving his Son as a sacrifice for our sins. He did this so that the just requirement of the law would be fully satisfied for us, who no longer follow our sinful nature but instead follow the Spirit.

Those who are dominated by the sinful nature think about sinful things, but those who are controlled by the Holy Spirit think about things that please the Spirit. So letting your sinful nature control your mind leads to death. But letting the Spirit control your mind leads to life and peace.

For the sinful nature is always hostile to God. It never did obey God's laws, and it never will. That's why those who are still under the control of their sinful nature can never please God.

But you are not controlled by your sinful nature. You are controlled by the Spirit if you have the Spirit of God living in you. (And remember that those who do not have the Spirit of Christ living in them do not belong to him at all.) And Christ lives within you, so even though your body will die because of sin, the Spirit gives you life because you have been made right with God. The Spirit of God, who raised Jesus from the dead, lives in you. And just as God raised Christ Jesus from the dead, he will give life to your mortal bodies by this same Spirit living within you.

Therefore, dear brothers and sisters, you have no obligation to do what your sinful nature urges you to do. For if you live by its dictates, you will die. But if through the power of the Spirit you put to death the deeds of your sinful nature, you will live. For all who are led by the Spirit of God are children of God.

So you have not received a spirit that makes you fearful slaves. Instead, you received God's Spirit when he adopted you as his own children. Now we call him, Abba, Father. For his Spirit joins with our spirit to affirm that we are God's children. And since we are his children, we are his heirs. In fact, together with Christ we are heirs of God's glory. But if we are to share his glory, we must also share his suffering.

Yet what we suffer now is nothing compared to the glory he will reveal to us later. For all creation is waiting eagerly for that future day when God will reveal who his children really are. Against its will, all creation was subjected to God's curse. But with eager hope, the creation looks forward to the day when it will join God's children in glorious freedom from death and decay. For we know that all creation has been groaning as in the pains of childbirth right up to the present time.

And we believers also groan, even though we have the Holy Spirit within us as a foretaste of future glory, for we long for our bodies to be released from sin and suffering. We, too, wait with eager hope for the day when God will give us our full rights as his adopted children, including the new bodies he has promised us. We were given this hope when we were saved. (If we already have something, we don't need to hope for it. But if we look forward to something we don't yet have, we must wait patiently and confidently.)

And the Holy Spirit helps us in our weakness. For example, we don't know what God wants us to pray for. But the Holy Spirit prays for us with groanings that cannot be expressed in words. And the Father who knows all hearts knows what the Spirit is saying, for the Spirit pleads for us believers in harmony with God's own will. And we know that God causes everything to work together for the good of those who love God and are called according to his purpose for them.

For God knew his people in advance, and he chose them to become like his Son, so that his Son would be the firstborn among many brothers and sisters. And having chosen them, he called them to come to him. And having called them, he gave them right standing with himself. And having given them right standing, he gave them his glory.

What shall we say about such wonderful things as these? If God is for us, who can ever be against us? Since he did not spare even his own Son but gave him up for us all, won't he also give us everything else? Who dares accuse us whom God has chosen for his own? No one—for God himself has given us right standing with himself. Who then will condemn us? No one—for Christ Jesus died for us and was raised to life for us, and he is sitting in the place of honor at God's right hand, pleading for us.

That Old Rugged Cross

I am sure you have heard of the old rugged cross before. My mom used to talk about the cross all the time. In fact, my husband and I have many crosses up in our house as a show of love for God. They symbolize Jesus dying on the cross for our sins.

1 Corinthians 1:24-25 –But to those called by God to salvation, both Jews and Gentiles, Christ is the power of God and the wisdom of God. This foolish plan of God is wiser than the wisest of human plans and God's weakness is stronger than the greatest of human strength.

1 Corinthians 1:30-31 – God has united you with Christ Jesus. For our benefit God made him to be wisdom itself. Christ made us right with God; he made us pure and holy, and he freed us from sin. Therefore, as the Scriptures say, if you want to boast, boast only about the Lord.

Hebrews 12:2 – We do this by keeping our eyes on Jesus, the champion who initiates and perfects our faith. Because of the joy awaiting him, he endured the cross, disregarding its shame. Now he is seated in the place of honor beside God's throne.

1 John 5:6 – And Jesus Christ was revealed as God's Son by his baptism in water and by shedding his blood on the cross – not by water only, but by water and blood. And the Spirit, who is truth, confirms it with his testimony.

Let's Talk About Love

We all know about love. We love our parents, our children, our families, our pets. We love God. But nothing can compare to God's love for us.

Here is what the Bible says about love.

1 Corinthians 13

If I could speak all the languages of earth and of angels, but didn't love others, I would only be a noisy gong or a clanging cymbal. If I had the gift of prophecy, and if I understood all of God's secret plans and possessed all knowledge, and if I had such faith that I could move mountains, but didn't love others, I would be nothing. If I gave everything I have to the poor and even sacrificed my body, I could boast about it; but if I didn't love others, I would have gained nothing.

Love is patient and kind. Love is not jealous or boastful or proud or rude. It does not demand its own way. It is not irritable, and it keeps no record of being wronged. It does not rejoice about injustice but rejoices whenever the truth wins out. Love never gives up, never loses faith, is always hopeful, and endures through every circumstance.

Prophecy and speaking in unknown languages and special knowledge will become useless. But love will last forever! Now our knowledge is partial and incomplete, and even the gift of prophecy reveals only part of the whole picture! But when the time of perfection comes, these partial things will become useless.

When I was a child, I spoke and thought and reasoned as a child. But when I grew up, I put away childish things. Now we see things imperfectly, like puzzling reflections in a mirror, but then we will see everything with perfect clarity. All that I know now is partial and incomplete, but then I will know everything completely, just as God now knows me completely.

Three things will last forever—faith, hope, and love—and the greatest of these is love.

1 John 3:1 – See how very much our Father loves us, for he calls us his children, and that is what we are! But the people who belong to this world don't recognize that we are God's children because they don't know him.

Romans 5:5 – And this hope will not lead to disappointment. For we know how dearly God loves us, because he has given us the Holy Spirit to fill our hearts with this love.

1 John 4:16 – We know how much God loves us, and we have put our trust in his love. God is love, and all who live in love live in God, and God lives in them.

Keep Your Eyes On The Prize

We must keep our eyes on the prize. Did I mention that there would be a prize? Something to look forward to? Something so spectacular that you could not even picture it? I will cover this more a little later on, but here is a sneak peek…

Living With God In Heaven Forever !!

1 Peter 2:11 – We are not happy here because we are not at home here. We are not happy here because we are not supposed to be happy here. We are like foreigners and strangers in this world.

2 Timothy 4:7-8 – I have done my best in the race, I have run the full distance and I have kept the faith. And now there is waiting for me the victory prize of being put right with God, which the Lord, the righteous Judge, will give me on that Day – and not only to me, but to all those who wait with love for him to appear.

2 Peter 3:11-14 – Since everything around us is going to be destroyed like this, what holy and godly lives you should live, looking forward to the day of God and hurrying it along. On that day, he will set the heavens on fire and the elements will melt away in the flames. But we are looking forward to the new heavens and the new earth he has promised, a world filled with God's righteousness.

And so, dear friends, while you are waiting for these things to happen, make every effort to be found living peaceful lives that are pure and blameless in his sight.

John 14:1-3 – Don't let your hearts be troubled. Trust in God and trust also in me. There is more than enough room in my Father's home. If this were not so, would I have told you that I am going to prepare a place for you? When everything is ready, I will come and get you, so that you will always be with me where I am.

Psalm 117:1-2 – Praise the Lord, all you nations. Praise him, all you people of the earth. For his unfailing love for us is powerful; the Lord's faithfulness endures forever. Praise the Lord!

Psalm 121:1-8 – I look up to the mountains – does my help come from there? My help comes from the Lord, who made heaven and earth!

He will not let you stumble; the one who watches over you will not slumber. Indeed, he who watches over Israel never slumbers or sleeps.

The Lord himself watches over you! The Lord stands beside you as your protective shade. The sun will not harm you by day, nor the moon by night.

The Lord keeps you from all harm and watches over your life. The Lord keeps watch over you as you come and go, both now and forever.

Jesus Is In Control And He Is Coming Back !!

Although it does not seem it all the time, Jesus is in control. Believe me, you will want to pay attention to this statement. Wait until you see what is coming in the future.

Matthew 28:18 – All authority in heaven and on earth has been given to me.

Matthew 11:27 – All things have been handed over to me by my Father.

Remember, Jesus defeated the devil when he died on the cross for our sins.

He knows what our talents are and what is best for our lives. I don't know about you, but life can be so hard and confusing. Thank you God for having control. We have control over nothing, except how we react to situations.

Psalm 32:8 – The Lord says, I will guide you along the best pathway for your life. I will advise you and watch over you.

Isaiah 26:4 – Trust in the Lord always, for the Lord God is the eternal rock.

Isaiah 30:18 – So the Lord must wait for you to come to him so he can show you his love and compassion. For the Lord is a faithful God. Blessed are those who wait for his help.

Jesus will be returning in all His glory. Can you guess that this is one of my favorite things to talk about?

Zechariah 1:6 – On that day the sources of light will no longer shine, yet there will be continuous day! Only the Lord knows how this could happen. There will be no normal day and night, for at evening time it will still be light.

2 Peter 3:13 – But we are looking forward to the new heavens and new earth he has promised, a world filled with God's righteousness.

2 Corinthians 5:2 – We grow weary in our present bodies, and we long to put on our heavenly bodies like new clothing.

Isaiah 65:17 – Look! I am creating new heavens and a new earth, and no one will even think about the old ones anymore.

1 Thessalonians 4:14 – For since we believe that Jesus died and was raised to life again, we also believe that when Jesus returns, God will bring back with him the believers who have died.

Acts 1:11 – Men of Galilee, they said, why are you standing here staring into heaven? Jesus has been taken from you into heaven, but someday he will return from heaven in the same way you saw him go!

CHAPTER 4
Life Is Not Easy

Zeus – Our Adventure Bunny

Forgive Others

Uggg.. this is the worst. If you only knew how many people disappointed me, hurt me – mentally and emotionally, mean, evil, nasty people, there was a lot. I love animals. People – I could do without a lot of them. But, I have to live with people and they are only human and not perfect. I am not perfect either and God forgave me. So I have to forgive them.

If Jesus could forgive his enemies, I can too. I am kicking a rock like a child while I type this, I am so stubborn. I really want to hurt those that hurt me. But, I do need to forgive. So to everyone who has ever hurt, disappointed or been mean to myself, my husband Kerry or my parents, I forgive you. Now, I just need to work on those that will do the same to us in the future. I am a work in progress. I am only human. But, I will forgive them.

Luke 23:34 – Father, forgive them; they don't know what they are doing.

Ephesians 6:18 – Prayer is essential in this ongoing warfare. Pray long and hard. Pray for your brothers and your sisters.

Matthew 6:15 – But if you refuse to forgive others, you Father will not forgive your sins.

Luke 6:37 – Do not judge others, and you will not be judged. Do not condemn others, or it will all come back against you. Forgive others and you will be forgiven.

Colossians 3:13 – *Make allowance for each other's faults and forgive anyone who offends you. Remember, the Lord forgave you, so you must forgive others.*

1 Samuel 15:25 – *But now, please forgive my sin and come back with me so that I may worship the Lord.*

Luke 17:4 – *Even if that person wrongs you seven times a day and each time turns again and asks forgiveness, you must forgive.*

Proverbs 17:9 – *Love prospers when a fault is forgiven, but dwelling on it separates close friends.*

To those individuals who hurt, disappointed, were cruel or mean to myself, my husband, or any of my family members and to those who continue to be cruel or mean to others, I hope that you find God before it is too late. You know who you are!

When God Says No

God already knows what is going to happen, what we are going to do, what stupid things we are going to say. Just when I think I won't mess things up, oops there I go again. But, as long as I confess my sin and what I did (and really mean that I am sorry), God will forgive me. Thank you to Jesus for dying for our sins.

I pray and I have waited for an answer. Some of my prayers I am still waiting for an answer – it's been years. I get frustrated, I get irritated, I wonder if I am praying right or asking for the right thing. Then I want to give up. What's the point? I feel like I am talking to myself. I do enough of that at work. Makes people think I am crazy.

So what do I do now? God must be saying no. But maybe the answer will eventually be yes. I need to have faith that God is in control. I have to be content that God will lead me in the right direction and provide an answer. It might not be what I want, but He knows best.

Psalm 46:10 – Be still and know that I am God.

In the middle of the storms of life, I am going to be still and focus on God. I am going to be quiet (which is not easy for me – I am loud and laugh even louder). I am going to be open and will trust God. I am going to pray non-stop.

We have to trust that God knows what is better for us, even when the answer is no. We cannot see what God sees, we cannot know what He knows. He will do what is best for us.

Proverbs 3:5-6 – Trust in the Lord with all your heart; do not depend on your own understanding. Seek his will in all you do, and he will show you which path to take.

Psalm 31:14 – But I am trusting you, O Lord, saying – You are my God!

Palm 52:8 – But I am like an olive tree, thriving in the house of God. I will always trust in God's unfailing love.

Isaiah 26:4 – Trust in the Lord always, for the Lord God is the eternal Rock.

John 12:44 – Jesus shouted to the crowds – if you trust me, you are trusting not only me, but also God who sent me.

John 14:1 – Don't let your hearts be troubled. Trust in God, and trust also in me.

2 Timothy 3:15 – You have been taught the Holy Scriptures from childhood, and they have given you the wisdom to receive the salvation that comes by trusting in Christ Jesus.

My Big Plans

I had these elaborate plans to become a screenwriter. I bought the script writing program, I wrote scripts, I faxed out my introductory letter, I even had a professional script writer read my scripts. I did as much I could possibly think to do. But it never went anywhere. But still the characters and the stories kept coming to me. I had to write them down to get them out of my head. I believe that God gave me a gift for writing. But my grand plans, have not gotten anywhere.

Then I realized that maybe the timing was not right. I will get my stories out there someday when God lets me know when to do it. God had other plans for me. I had to go through the experiences, perform caretaking duties, hold down a regular job, and then come back to God. It all happened for a reason. After I lost my mom, I got the idea and push from God to write this book. Maybe this is the beginning of my writing career. Whatever the outcome, I am trusting God to use me to, hopefully, get His Word out and help others.

I have to trust God's plan over my plans.

Proverbs 16:1-3 – We can make our own plans, but the Lord gives the right answer. People may be pure in their own eyes, but the Lord examines their motives. Commit your actions to the Lord, and your plans will succeed.

Ecclesiastes 6:10 – Everything has already been decided. It was known long ago what each person would be. So there is no use arguing with God about your destiny.

We All Have Gifts

As I stated earlier, one of the gifts I believe I received from God is my ability to create and write. I love words and I can picture scenes and characters and whole stories in my mind. I like to think that I have other gifts as well – gift of caring, gift of helping, gift of encouragement. What gifts do you have? Take a moment and think about that.

Romans 12:6-8 – In his grace, God has given us different gifts for doing certain things well. So, if God has given you the ability to prophesy, speak out with as much faith as God has given you. If your gift is serving others, serve them well. If you are a teacher, teach well. If your gift is to encourage others, be encouraging. If it is giving, give generously. If God has given you leadership ability, take the responsibility seriously. And if you have a gift of showing kindness to others, do it gladly.

Romans 12:17 – Never pay back evil with more evil. Do things in such a way that everyone can see you are honorable. Do all that you can to live in peace with everyone.

Isn't it nice to know that we even have spiritual gifts? Read on...

1 Corinthians 12:4-9 – There are different kinds of spiritual gifts, but the same Spirit is the source of them all. There are different kinds of service, but we serve the same Lord. God works in different ways, but it is the same God who does the work in all of us.

A spiritual gift is given to each of us so we can help each other. To one person the Spirit gives the ability to give wise advice, to another the same Spirit gives a message of special knowledge. The same Spirit gives great faith to another and to someone else the one Spirit gives the gift of healing.

1 Peter 4:10 – God has given each of you a gift from his great variety of spiritual gifts. Use them well to serve one another.

Ecclesiastes 3:13 – And people should eat and drink and enjoy the fruits of their labor, for these are gifts from God.

Numbers 18:29 – Be sure to give to the Lord the best portions of the gifts given to you.

Romans 1:11 – For I long to visit you so I can bring you some spiritual gift that will help you grow strong in the Lord.

2 Timothy 1:6 – This is why I remind you to fan into flames the spiritual gift God gave you when I laid my hands on you.

Focus On God

Well, I prayed and no answer seems to come. I can't sleep, I am anxious, I am discouraged.

What is next? How do I get through this? God has the answer.

Matthew 11:28 – Come to me all of you who are weary and carry heavy burdens and I will give you rest.

Psalm 25:15 – My eyes are always on the Lord, for he rescues me from the traps of my enemies.

Psalm 63:6-8 – I lie awake thinking of you, meditating on you through the night. Because you are my helper, I sing for joy in the shadow of your wings. I cling to you; your strong right hand holds me securely.

God knows our hearts. Maybe He sees our compassion, our devotion, our tenderness towards others. And what should we do? We should keep our focus on God.

When I get scared, frustrated, angry, when I cannot sleep and I feel like the devil is after me, I stop, take a breath and focus on God.

My mom taught me something when I was small that I still use to this day. I have trouble sleeping sometimes. I will find myself waking up, almost panicking in the middle of the night. I feel like my problems are overwhelming me. So, how do I go back to sleep? I focus on God.

I close my eyes and take my invisible blanket (the one in my mind) and I ask God if I can lay my blanket next to His throne (where He is sitting). I am not worthy to even lay by His sandal but He lets me. So, I lay may blanket down, ask God to protect me and then I go to sleep. It seems to work every time. Even in sleep, I focus on God.

I Samuel 16:7 – The Lord does not look at the things man looks at. Man looks at the outward appearance, but the Lord looks at the heart.

Hebrews 12:2 – We do this by keeping our eyes on Jesus, the champion who initiates and perfects our faith. Because of the joy awaiting him, he endured the cross, disregarding its shame. Now he is seated in the place of honor beside God's throne.

Psalm 123:2 – We keep looking to the Lord our God for his mercy, just as servants keep their eyes on their master, as a slave girl watches her mistress for the slightest signal.

2 Samuel 22:32 – For who is God except the Lord? Who but our God is a solid rock?

2 Samuel 22:3 – My God is my rock, in whom I find protection. He is my shield, the power that saves me, and my place of safety. He is my refuge, my savior, the one who saves me from violence.

Job 11:18 – Having hope will give you courage. You will be protected and will rest in safety.

Our One True Best Friend

Remember this, God is our one true best friend. Mom was my earthbound best friend and we shared a lot. My husband is my other earthbound best friend. But mom always told me that my one true best friend, the one who would never let me down and love me no matter what, was God. Again, she was right. I will say it again so you do not miss it. God is our one true best friend. Nothing can separate us from Him. Thank you, God!

Romans 8:38-39 – Neither death, nor life, nor angels, nor ruling spirits; nothing now, nothing in the future, no powers, nothing above us, nothing below us, nor anything else in the world will ever be able to separate us from the love of God that is in Christ Jesus our Lord.

Isaiah 55:8-9 – My thoughts are not like your thoughts. Your ways are not like my ways. Just as the heavens are higher than the earth, so are my ways higher than your ways and my thoughts higher than your thoughts.

Proverbs 3:11-12 – My child, don't reject the Lord's discipline, and don't be upset when he corrects you. For the Lord corrects those he loves, just as a father corrects a child in whom he delights.

Deuteronomy 33:27 – The eternal God is your refuge, and his everlasting arms are under you. He drives out the enemy before you; he cries out – Destroy them!

Friends And Extended Family on Earth

I have been very fortunate to meet some amazing people on this earth. Some of them are acquaintances and some are friends. Some are my extended family.

One friend I would like to mention, Pastor William Kent Collins, Sr., has been my co-worker for many years and I am proud to say my friend. He has been a mentor to me. When I was angry, confused, crying, depressed, William never let me down. He was always there for me especially when I needed to be reminded that God was in control. William always has a Bible verse or an inspirational Bible story ready to help me. Besides my mother, William always told me to never give up on God.

A little note about Pastor William Kent Collins, Sr. William is the Pastor for Spiritual Life Family Worship Center, SpiritualLifeFWC@gmail.com. William is also the author of inspirational books. If anyone gets the chance, please read "The Flat Family Series". *The Flat Family Series is a collection of short stories that will encourage creativity, boost self-esteem, and promote the value of difference.*

My husband was raised by two wonderful people, besides his terrific mom. They are his nanny, Nette, her husband Dickie who is a pastor, and our two "sisters" - Gracie and Marjorie. Nette and Dickie have always provided Kerry (and myself) a loving, God-filled extended family. Thank you and we love you always. You never gave up on us.

Gracie and Marjorie are our extended sisters (in life and in God) and we love you. Thank you for your support and for always being there for us.

Being surrounded by people who love God has been an amazing gift. God has blessed my husband and myself with an extended family. We are truly grateful. They have been instrumental in keeping our focus on God.

I wish I had the space to thank all the people who have been important in my life and that I love dearly. They know who they are – so I am thanking them here for everything they did for me now and in the future. God bless all of you.

There are too many to list, but I am going to give a shout out to a few very special people ...

Robert (Bev and Travis) – thank you for being my brother on this earth. You have always been there when I needed you. The faith you have in God has kept me lifted when I needed it. Robert – you have the best sense of humor and you really should have been a comedian.

Brad – such a blessing added to our life. Your faith in God and your friendship is something we will treasure forever.

Jill & Marc – you both know that you are special to us and we love you lots. Your friendship and support means the world to us. God blessed us with you.

Pete & Deb – thank you for your love, support, and friendship. You have been a true blessing from God. You will always be a part of our family.

Rita – my sister whom I have always looked up to since childhood. You are a good person and your faith and love of God is a beautiful gift that you will be able to pass along to many people. I love you very much.

CHAPTER 5
A Grand Future

Mom & Dad

A New Home

John 14:1-4 – Don't let your hearts be troubled. Trust in God, and trust in me. There are many rooms in my Father's house. I would not tell you this if it were not true. I am going there to prepare a place for you. After I go and prepare a place for you, I will come back and take you to be with me so that you may be where I am.

I don't know about you, but I get so excited when I read this scripture. Wow – we have a home to go to. It will be so great. It is beyond our comprehension that we will be with God, our loved ones, our pets. We will be living with and praising God (our creator). Is there anything better than this? I don't think so.

We can't even imagine how glorious it is going to be…..

1 Corinthians 2:9 – No one has ever imagined what God has prepared for those who love him.

Psalm 84:1-4 – How lovely is your dwelling place, O Lord of Heaven's Armies. I long, yes I faint with longing to enter the courts of the Lord. With my whole being, body and soul, I will shout joyfully to the living God. Even the sparrow finds a home and the swallow builds her nest and raises her young at a place near your altar, O Lord of Heaven's Armies, my King and my God! What joy for those who can live in your house, always singing your praises.

Psalm 84:10-12 – A single day in your courts is better than a thousand anywhere else! I would rather be a gatekeeper in the house of my God than live the good life in the homes of the wicked. For the Lord is our sun and our shield. He gives us grace and glory. The Lord will withhold no good thing from those who do what is right. O Lord of Heaven's Armies, what joy for those who trust in you.

Isaiah 60:19-21 – No longer will you need the sun to shine by day nor the moon to give its light by night, for the Lord your God will be your everlasting light, and your God will be your glory. Your sun will never set; your moon will not go down. For the Lord will be your everlasting light. Your days of mourning will come to an end.

I am looking forward to the new heaven and the new earth. What a marvelous place it will be for all of us. We will all be together again.

Isaiah 65:17-19 – Look! I am creating new heavens and a new earth, and no one will even think about the old ones anymore. Be glad; rejoice forever in my creation! And look, I will create Jerusalem as a place of happiness. Her people will be a source of joy. I will rejoice over Jerusalem and delight in my people. And the sound of weeping and crying will be heard in it no more.

Even the animals will get along with each other.

Isaiah 65:25 – The wolf and the lamb will feed together. The lion will eat hay like a cow. But the snakes will eat dust. In those days no one will be hurt or destroyed on my holy mountain. I, the Lord, have spoken!*

Check this out…. What hope we have !

Micah 4:1- In the last days, the mountain of the Lord's house will be the highest of all….the most important place on earth. It will be raised above the other hills, and people from all over the world will stream there to worship.

Micah 4:4 – Everyone will live in peace and prosperity, enjoying their own grapevines and fig trees, for there will be nothing to fear. The Lord of Heaven's Armies has made this promise!

I Hope I Don't Screw It Up

One of my greatest fears growing up was that I was totally screwing everything up. I feel like I did with my parents and husband – although I guess I haven't screwed it up so bad, they still love me. But, my worst fear was that I would screw things up with God and He would totally reject me.

Look at my track record – I swore, I didn't read the Bible a lot, I acted like a jackass to a lot of people, I could be mean, even I couldn't stand me at times. I apologized to everyone but, I should have been able to handle things better.

But, after all these years and all my screw ups, God never gave up on me. I even got proof. When a family member was going through his cancer crisis and I asked for a sign that all would be okay, one dark and dreary morning he saw three pure white cats pass in front of his car on his way to work. This has never happened before or since. I knew immediately that the three pure white cats represented (at least to me) – the Father, Son and Holy Spirit. A complete peace came over me. I just knew all would be okay and it was.

My mom is always talking in my head saying to never give up hope in God. He forgives us and loves us, no matter what. Just keep praying, believing and trusting God.

I have thought about this for a long time. I have been a jerk in the past. I can be happy, funny, friendly and caring. But, because of sin, I have snapped at my loved ones, argued with those I cherish, I have felt guilty, ashamed, bitter, and angry. I have had sleepless nights and stress beyond belief.

But since Jesus died for me (and you) on the cross, all of that has been forgiven. And there is hope for the future. Nothing can separate us from the love of God.

Revelation 21:4 – God will wipe away every tear from their eyes, and there will be no more death, sadness, crying, or pain, because all the old ways are gone.

Romans 8:38-39 – I am sure that neither death nor life, nor angels, nor ruling spirits, nothing now, nothing in the future, no powers, nothing above us, nothing below us, nor anything else in the whole world will ever be able to separate us from the love of God that is in Christ Jesus our Lord.

I am a sinner. There, I said it. I am human and I will always sin. Thank you God for knowing my heart. Although I may backslide and make mistakes, God knows my heart. He knows yours too. That's a good thing.

Psalm 139:1-6 – O Lord, you have examined my heart and know everything about me. You know when I sit down or stand up. You know my thoughts even when I'm far away. You see me when I travel and when I rest at home. You know everything I do. You know what I am going to say even before I say it, Lord. You go before me and follow me. You place your hand of blessing on my head. Such knowledge is too wonderful for me, too great for me to understand.

Psalm 139:16 – You saw me before I was born. Every day of my life was recorded in your book. Every moment was laid out before a single day had passed.

My mom always said I was precious to her. That was full of love and so special to me. Can you imagine the amount of love and how special we are to God when he calls us precious? Love beyond belief.

Psalm 139:17-18 – How precious are your thoughts about me, O God. They cannot be numbered. I can't even count them; they outnumber the grains of sand. And when I wake up, you are still with me!

1 John 5:1 –Everyone who believes that Jesus is the Christ has become a child of God. And everyone who loves the Father loves his children, too.

Proverbs 3:12 – For the Lord corrects those he loves, just as a father corrects a child in whom he delights.

Hebrews 12:6 – For the Lord disciplines those he loves, and he punishes each one he accepts as his child.

Romans 8:31 – What shall we say about such wonderful things as these? If God is for us, who can ever be against us?

A Work In Progress

I fall short in a lot of ways, but I am trying. I want to be a better person and help others find God. I believe I will always be a work in progress, but if I can help one person love God and get into heaven then I will be happy.

I have never been a person that needs or wants praise or attention. I am very much a loner and I hate speaking in public, so maybe these words will help.

2 Peter 3:11-12 –So what kind of people should you be? You should live holy lives and serve God, as you wait for and look forward to the coming of the day of God.

I have a quick temper and I have to learn to reign it in sometimes. I have to keep reminding myself that God is watching at all times. I really don't want to make Him mad at me.

Psalm 33:13-15 – The Lord looks down from heaven and sees the whole human race. From his throne he observes all who live on the earth. He made their hearts so he understands everything they do.

Every time I make a mistake, I look for the lightning bolt. I fear that God will be so mad at me for this stupid act, that I will become dust. Because of Jesus, I know my sins are forgiven. Thank God for loving and forgiving us.

Proverbs 2:3-7 – Cry out for insight and ask for understanding. Search for them as you would for silver; seek them like hidden treasures.

Then you will understand what it means to fear the Lord, and you will gain knowledge of God. For the Lord grants wisdom. From his mouth come knowledge and understanding. He grants a treasure of common sense to the honest. He is a shield to those who walk with integrity.

From both my mom and dad, I was taught to show compassion and empathy towards people – even the mean ones. I will keep on trying to be nice. I am always loyal and protective towards my friends. I will not change this either.

Proverbs 3:3 – Never let loyalty and kindness leave you. Tie them around your neck as a reminder. Write them deep within your heart.

The way we live – the way we react to problems – the way we react to negativity, people watch. It is human nature. We want to see how others deal with their issues. Those of us who want to bring others to know, love, and believe in God have to do our best to shine for God – to bring the glory and honor to Him. It is not always easy, but it can be done.

Matthew 5:16 – In the same way, let your good deeds shine out for all to see, so that everyone will praise your heavenly Father.

All Praise, Glory, & Honor

My mom taught me to pray saying – all praise, glory and honor to the Father, in the name of Jesus through the Holy Spirit. I told you my mom was smart. She said to pray about everything and pray as much as I could. As I said earlier – pray, pray, pray. And praise God for everything.

We can never praise Him enough !!!! If you don't know what to say – read some of these Bible verses.

Psalm 34:1-3 – I will praise the Lord at all times. I will constantly speak his praises. I will boast only in the Lord; let all who are helpless take heart. Come, let us tell of the Lord's greatness; let us exalt his name together.

Psalm 47:2 – For the Lord Most High is awesome. He is the great King of all the earth.

Psalm 48:10 – As your name deserves, O God, you will be praised to the ends of the earth. Your strong right hand is filled with victory.

Psalm 57:5 – Be exalted, O God, above the highest heavens! May your glory shine over all the earth.

Psalm 66:1-4 – Shout joyful praises to God, all the earth! Sing about the glory of his name! Tell the world how glorious he is. Say to God, How awesome are your deeds! Your enemies cringe before your mighty power.

Everything on earth will worship you; they will sing your praises, shouting your name in glorious songs.

Psalm 69:34-36 – Praise him, O heaven and earth, the seas and all that move in them. For God will save Jerusalem and rebuild the towns of Judah. His people will live there and settle in their own land. The descendants of those who obey him will inherit the land, and those who love him will live there in safety.

Psalm 100 – Shout with joy to the Lord, all the earth! Worship the Lord with gladness. Come before him, singing with joy. Acknowledge that the Lord is God! He made us, and we are his. We are his people, the sheep of his pasture. Enter his gates with thanksgiving; go into his courts with praise. Give thanks to him and praise his name. For the Lord is good. His unfailing love continues forever, and his faithfulness continues to each generation.

Deuteronomy 10:21 – He alone is your God, the only one who is worthy of your praise, the one who has done these mighty miracles that you have seen with your own eyes.

2 Samuel 22:47 – The Lord lives! Praise to my Rock! May God, the Rock of my salvation, be exalted!

Our Father Rules The Universe

I loved my earthly dad. He had faults, as we all do. But, he loved God and his faith made him a great person.

But our Father in Heaven – now he is the awesome God and Father for all of us.

Look at what He made. The only words I can think of are "Wow, Incredible, Unbelievable, Awesome".

Psalm 19:1-5 – The heavens tell the glory of God and the skies announce what his hands have made. Day after day they tell the story; night after night they tell it again. They have no speech or words; they have no voice to be heard. But their message goes out through all the world; their words go everywhere on earth.

Job 38:16, 22; 39:19-20, 26 – Have you ever gone to where the sea begins or walked the valleys under the sea?......Have you ever gone to the storehouse for snow or seen the storehouses for hail...? Are you the one who gives the horse his strength or puts the flowing mane on its neck? Do you make the horse jump like a locust? Is it through your wisdom that the hawk flies and spreads its wings toward the south?

Gosh, what can I say about this? How I have always loved the magnificent horse. I always wanted a white horse. Or the beautiful rainbows (God's covenant with Noah), or any of the beauty of nature? A storehouse for snow or hail? God made everything. I cannot even draw a stick figure. All Praise, Glory and Honor to you Almighty Father – forever and ever.

CHAPTER 6

From Rainbows to Owls

Nina – Our Baby

Rainbows

Ever since I was a child I have been fascinated by rainbows. The translucent colors in the sky after a rain made me smile. They are so uplifting. Even finding a rainbow in a puddle, or in a prism stops you in your tracks. Nothing compares to the colors of a rainbow.

Finding out about God's promise to never flood the world again with his rainbow covenant really makes them special.

Genesis 9:13- I have placed my rainbow in the cloud. It is the sign of my covenant with you and with all the earth. When I send clouds over the earth, the rainbow will appear in the clouds. When I see the rainbow in the clouds, I will remember the eternal covenant between God and every living creature on earth. Then God said to Noah –Yes, this rainbow is the sign of the covenant I am confirming with all the creatures on earth.

The rainbow does not just exist on the earth either. When we get to Heaven we will see another rainbow.

Revelation 4:3 – The one sitting on the throne was as brilliant as gemstones – like jasper and carnelian. And the glow of an emerald circled his throne like a rainbow.

Revelation 10:1 – Then I saw another mighty angel coming down from heaven, surrounded by a cloud, with a rainbow over his head. His face shone like the sun, and his feet were like pillars of fire.

Look At God's Creations and Be Amazed

Just look anywhere and you will see what God created – which is everything. What an awesome God. The amazing trees, the beautiful rainbow, the skies, the sea, the flowers, animals, the person next to you.

Psalm 33:6-9 – The Lord merely spoke, and the heavens were created. He breathed the word, and all the stars were born. He assigned the seas its boundaries and locked the oceans in vast reservoirs. Let the whole world fear the Lord, and let everyone stand in awe of him. For when he spoke, the world began! It appeared at his command.

Psalm 77:16-19 – When the Red Sea saw you, O God, its waters looked and trembled! The sea quaked to its very depths. The clouds poured down rain; the thunder rumbled in the sky. Your arrows of lightning flashed. Your thunder roared from the whirlwind; the lightning lit up the world! The earth trembled and shook. Your road let through the sea, your pathway through the mighty waters – a pathway no one knew was there!

Isaiah 40:12-13 – Who else has held the oceans in his hand? Who has measured off the heavens with his fingers? Who else knows the weight of the earth or has weighed the mountains and hills on a scale? Who is able to advise the Spirit of the Lord? Who knows enough to give him advice or teach him?

Isaiah 40:15 – For all the nations of the world are but a drop in the bucket. They are nothing more than dust on the scales. He picks up the whole earth as though it were a grain of sand.

Colossians 1:17 –He existed before anything else, and he holds all creation together.

Romans 8:19 –For all creation is waiting eagerly for that future day when God will reveal who his children really are.

Psalm 145:9 – The Lord is good to everyone. He showers compassion on all his creation.

Psalm 104:24 – O Lord, what a variety of things you have made! In wisdom you have made them all. The earth is full of your creatures.

Genesis 9:17 –Then God said to Noah, Yes this rainbow is the sign of the covenant I am confirming with all the creatures on earth.

Psalm 145:9 – The Lord is good to everyone. He showers compassion on all his creations.

The Importance & Love of Animals

I love animals so much that I have been known to cry when I see a dead animal on the street - squirrel, bird, they all matter to me. One time at work I saw a sea gull getting attacked by another bird. I chased the bird off, grabbed the hurt sea gull and cradled it on my lap while a co-worker rushed myself (crying) with the injured bird to my vet (who is awesome – compassionate and so talented). However, the sea gull passed away on the way. I cried so hard, but I knew I did the right thing in trying to save the bird. That bird is in heaven waiting for me. I know we will be reunited. I can hardly wait – that bird is getting a big hug from me.

Okay, this one will sound crazy. I save bugs. Not spiders or biting insects (wasps, bees, etc.). Those I cannot be sure of and I don't want anyone to get hurt. But other bugs – well I catch them and release them outside. I am sure others do this, right?

God loves animals, birds, and insects, all of creation. God created everything so he loves everything. I know that I will see all of my pets and the many, many, many, deceased animals I have seen on the street and asked that when I make it to heaven they become my pets. I am going to have so many pets I will need my own wing in Heaven. My mom and I always wanted our own menagerie of pets, someday we will.

Psalm 36:6 – Your righteousness is like the mighty mountains, your justice like the ocean depths. You care for people and animals alike, O, Lord.

We Are God's Sheep

Like I said, I got my love for animals from my mother. They always have been and always will be special to me. My mom always called me her "little chickie" and always told me that we were God's sheep. So, along with a lot of people, I love the below Bible verse.

Not only does it say that God is our Shepherd, it also talks about our future home in heaven. And we get to praise His name.

Psalm 23 – The Lord is my shepherd; I have all that I need. He lets me rest in green meadows he leads me beside peaceful streams. He renews my strength. He guides me along right paths, bringing honor to his name. Even when I walk through the darkest valley, I will not be afraid, for you are close beside me. Your rod and your staff protect and comfort me. You prepare a feast for me in the presence of my enemies. You honor me by anointing my head with oil. My cup overflows with blessings. Surely your goodness and unfailing love will pursue me all the days of my life, and I will live in the house of the Lord forever.

God loves us so much he gives us chance after chance. What an awesome God.

Psalm 95:6-7 – Come, let us worship and bow down. Let us kneel before the Lord our maker, for he is our God. We are the people he watches over, the flock under his care.

Will I See My Pets Again?

I know in my heart that we will see our pets again. Thank God because I love and treasure each one of them. From the dog I had when I was a child, to the bunnies and all my pet fish (yes, even them), I will be so excited to be greeted by them when I get to the other side.

Animals (creatures) are innocent. They were, unfortunately, caught up in the corruption of man's sins.

Romans 8:18-21 – Yet what we suffer now is nothing compared to the glory he will reveal to us later. For all creation is waiting eagerly for that future day when God will reveal who his children really are. Against its will, all creation was subjected to God's curse. But with eager hope, the creation looks forward to the day when it will join God's children in glorious freedom from death and decay.

Even the animals will be praising God.

Revelations 5:13 – And then I heard every creature in heaven and on earth and under the earth and in the sea. They sang – blessing and honor and glory and power belong to the one sitting on the throne and to the Lamb forever and ever.

The animals, fish and birds already know about God. They really are smarter than we are in a lot of ways. They just can't talk.

Job 12:7-10 – Just ask the animals, and they will teach you. Ask the birds of the sky and they will tell you. Speak to the earth, and it will instruct you. Let the fish in the sea speak to you. For they all know that my disaster has come from the hand of the Lord. For the life of every living thing is in his hand and the breath of every human being.*

I know you have heard that animals can recognize and see spirits that we cannot see. Animals never sinned so they were never separated from God. They are in tune with nature. They know when storms are coming. Or when an earthquake is about to hit. They know. How many times have animals saved the lives of their owners? How many are trained to help those with sicknesses or disabilities?

Psalm 36:6 – Your righteousness is like the mighty mountains, your justice like the ocean depths. You care for people and animals alike, O Lord.

Matthew 10:29 – What is the price of two sparrows – one copper coin. But not a single sparrow can fall to the ground without your Father knowing it.

Psalm 145:9 – The Lord is good to everyone. He shows compassion on all his creation.

Want more proof that animals will be in heaven....

Isaiah 11:6 – In that day the wolf and the lamb will live together; the leopard will lie down with a baby goat. The calf and the yearling will be safe with the lion, and a little child will lead them all.

Be Wise – Like An Owl

There are so many Bible verses that provide a lot of wisdom that we can use in our everyday lives. Here are some of my favorites. Like a wise owl, read the Bible. See which ones are your favorites.

Proverbs 1:1-7 – These are the proverbs of Solomon, David's son, king of Israel. Their purpose is to teach people wisdom and discipline, to help them understand the insights of the wise. Their purpose is to teach people to live disciplined and successful lives, to help them do what is right, just, and fair. These proverbs will give insight to the simple, knowledge, and discernment to the young. Let the wise listen to these proverbs and become even wiser. Let those with understanding receive guidance by exploring the meaning in these proverbs and parables, the words of the wise and their riddles. Fear of the Lord is the foundation of true knowledge, but fools despise wisdom and discipline.

Listen to your mom and dad – they know what is best. Someday you may be a mom or a dad, so learn all the right things that you can. Make the world a better place. Make sure your foundation is God.

Proverbs 1:8-9 – My child, listen when your father corrects you. Don't neglect your mother's instruction. What you learn from them will crown you with grace and be a chain of honor around your neck.

God grants wisdom. Like a hidden treasure, wisdom will make your life better - honest, faithful and good.

Proverbs 2:3-8 – Cry out for insight and ask for understanding. Search for them as you would for silver; seek them like hidden treasures. Then you will understand what it means to fear the Lord, and you will gain knowledge of God. For the Lord grants wisdom.

From his mouth come knowledge and understanding. He grants a treasure of common sense to the honest. He is a shield to those who walk with integrity. He guards the paths of the just and protects those who are faithful to him.

Job 9:4 – For God is so wise and so mighty. Who has ever challenged him successfully?

Job 28:28 – And this is what he says to all humanity – the fear of the Lord is true wisdom; to forsake evil is real understanding.

Job 12:13 – But true wisdom and power are found in God; counsel and understanding are his.

1 Chronicles 22:12 – And may the Lord give you wisdom and understanding, that you may obey the Law of the Lord your God as you rule over Israel.

Exodus 31:3 – I have filled him with the Spirit of God, giving him great wisdom, ability, and expertise in all kinds of crafts.

CHAPTER 7

Hide Me Under Your Wings

Goldfinches In Our Yard

Some Proverb & Psalm One Liners

Psalm and Proverbs both have a wealth of sayings to help you throughout your life. Here are some that I like to remember.

Proverbs 10:9 – People with integrity walk safely, but those who follow crooked paths will be exposed.

Proverbs 10:12 – Hatred stirs up quarrels, but love makes up for all offenses.

Proverbs 10:14 – Wise people treasure knowledge, but the babbling of a fool invites disaster.

Proverbs 10:17 – People who accept discipline are on the pathway to life, but those who ignore correction will go astray.

Proverbs 10:19 – Too much talk leads to sin. Be sensible and keep your mouth shut.

Proverbs 10:25 – When the storms of life come, the wicked are whirled away, but the godly have a lasting foundation.

Proverbs 11:4 – Riches won't help on the day of judgement, but right living can save you from death.

Proverbs – 11:17 – Your kindness will reward you, but your cruelty will destroy you.

Proverbs 12:19 – Truthful words stand the test of time, but lies are soon exposed.

Proverbs 13:20 – Walk with the wise and become wise; associate with fools and get in trouble.

Proverbs 29:6 – Evil people are trapped by sin, but the righteous escape, shouting for joy.

Psalm 5:3 – Listen to my voice in the morning, Lord. Each morning I bring my requests to you and wait expectantly.

Psalm 9:1-2 – I will praise you, Lord, with all my heart; I will tell of all the marvelous things you have done. I will be filled with joy because of you. I will sing praises to your name, O Most High.

Psalm 18:30 – God's way is perfect. All the Lord's promises prove true. He is a shield for all who look to him for protection.

Psalm 27:1 – The Lord is my light and my salvation – so why should I be afraid?

Psalm 62:2 – He alone is my rock and my salvation, my fortress where I will never be shaken.

Psalm 97:6 – The heavens proclaim his righteousness; every nation sees his glory.

There are so many more that can help you, take a moment and read all of Psalm and Proverbs.

Angels Watching Over Us
Or
"Cool, I Have My Own Angel"

There has been a lot written about and said about angels. But I believe what the Bible tells me…..

Psalm 91:11 – He has put his angels in charge of you to watch over you wherever you go.

Psalm 34:7 – For the angel of the Lord is a guard; he surrounds and defends all who fear him.

Psalm 103:19-22 – The Lord has made the heavens his throne; from there he rules over everything. Praise the Lord, you angels, you mighty ones who carry out his plans, listening for each of his commands. Yes, praise the Lord, you armies of angels who serve him and do his will. Praise the Lord, everything he has created, everything in all his kingdom.

Psalm 89:5-7 – All heaven will praise your great wonders, Lord; myriad of angels will praise you for your faithfulness. For who in all of heaven can compare with the Lord? What mightiest angel is anything like the Lord? The highest angelic powers stand in awe of God. He is far more awesome than all who surround his throne.

I know that angels exist. My mom told me that as a young girl she developed a large mass on her neck. It was huge. Doctors did not know what to do, but mom did.

She prayed and trusted God. She told me that an angel came to her and told her that she would be okay. The mass burst on its own, drained, and she was fine. After this happened she went out and bought her first Bible and read it non-stop. She never gave up on God. She loved Him so much. This experience helped my mom help others find God. She helped me find God.

Just because we cannot see angels, does not mean they do not exist. It is a spirit filled world.

Colossians 1:15-16 - Christ is the visible image of the invisible God. He existed before anything was created and is supreme over all creation, for through him God created everything in the heavenly realms and on earth. He made the things we can see and the things we cannot see – such as thrones, kingdoms, rulers, and authorities in the unseen world. Everything was created through him and for him.

Hebrews 1:14 – Therefore, angels are only servants – spirits sent to care for people who will inherit salvation.

Hebrews 12:22 – You have come to Mount Zion, to the city of the living God, the heavenly Jerusalem, and to countless thousands of angels in a joyful gathering.

Revelation 5:11 – Then I looked again, and I heard the voices of thousands and millions of angels around the throne and of the living beings and the elders.

Angels Are Neat – But Jesus Is Better

Do not make a mistake that angels are greater than Jesus. They are not !! Do not pray or worship angels. Jesus is the Son of God. Angels are his servants and messengers. There is only the Father, Son and Holy Spirit.

Hebrews 1 (in its entirety)

Long ago God spoke many times and in many ways to our ancestors through the prophets. And now in these final days, he has spoken to us through his Son. God promised everything to the Son as an inheritance and through the Son he created the universe.

The Son radiates God's own glory and expresses the very character of God and he sustains everything by the mighty power of his command. When he had cleansed us from our sins, he sat down in the place of honor at the right hand of the majestic God in heaven.

This shows that the Son is far greater than the angels, just as the name God gave him is greater than their names.

For God never said to any angel what he said to Jesus:

You are my Son, today I have become your Father.

God also said, I will be his Father and he will be my Son.

And when he brought his supreme Son into the world, God said, let all of God's angels worship him.

Regarding the angels, he says – he sends his angels like the winds, his servants like flames of fire.

But to the Son he says – Your throne, O God, endures forever and ever. You rule with a scepter of justice. You love justice and hate evil. Therefore, O God, your God has anointed you, pouring out the oil of joy on you more than on anyone else.

He also says to the Son – In the beginning, Lord, you laid the foundation of the earth and made the heavens with your hands.

They will perish, but you remain forever. They will wear out like old clothing. You will fold them up like a cloak and discard them like old clothing. But you are always the same, you will live forever.

And God never said to any of the angels – sit in the place of honor at my right hand until I humble your enemies, making them a footstool under your feet.

Therefore, angels are only servants – spirits sent to care for people who will inherit salvation.

Endure The Hard Times – Be Blessed

Nobody likes hard times, trials, or dealing with the everyday stresses. Sometimes I just want to put the pillow over my head and never leave the house again – just wait for Jesus to return. Unfortunately, life does not work that way. I know it is hard when we are being tested and treated terribly, but that is when you should try to shine the brightest and have faith.

But if we endure these trials and tribulations and patiently (as much as possible) wait and avoid evil temptations, we will be blessed. God said so and I believe Him.

James 1-2:18 -

Dear brothers and sisters, when troubles of any kind come your way, consider it an opportunity for great joy. For you know that when your faith is tested, your endurance has a chance to grow. So let it grow, for when your endurance is fully developed, you will be perfect and complete, needing nothing.

If you need wisdom, ask our generous God, and he will give it to you. He will not rebuke you for asking. But when you ask him, be sure that your faith is in God alone. Do not waver, for a person with divided loyalty is as unsettled as a wave of the sea that is blown and tossed by the wind. Such people should not expect to receive anything from the Lord. Their loyalty is divided between God and the world, and they are unstable in everything they do.

Believers who are poor have something to boast about, for God has honored them. And those who are rich should boast that God has humbled them. They will fade away like a little flower in the field. The hot sun rises and the grass withers; the little flower droops and falls, and its beauty fades away. In the same way, the rich will fade away with all of their achievements.

God blesses those who patiently endure testing and temptation. Afterward they will receive the crown of life that God has promised to those who love him. And remember, when you are being tempted, do not say, God is tempting me. God is never tempted to do wrong, and he never tempts anyone else. Temptation comes from our own desires, which entice us and drag us away.

These desires give birth to sinful actions. And when sin is allowed to grow, it gives birth to death.

So don't be misled, my dear brothers and sisters. Whatever is good and perfect is a gift coming down to us from God our Father, who created all the lights in the heavens. He never changes or casts a shifting shadow. He chose to give birth to us by giving us his true word. And we, out of all creation, became his prized possession.

Hide Me Under Your Wings

My mom always joked that she wanted to come back as a bird. After she passed away, I kept seeing yellow Goldfinches (female and male) and I find their pictures on so many things. Funny thing is, after she passed away, I found a picture of a yellow Goldfinch that my husband had put up behind the sofa where she sat all the time in our house. I had forgotten about the picture. I believe that is her symbol (and my dad's) that they are still with me. God brings peace to us in many ways.

My mom always told me she wanted to hide me under her arms which she called "wings" so I would not be hurt by the world or anyone in the world. She probably now has her wings as an angel of God. God will hide us under His wings and His wings are much stronger and everlasting.

Psalm 17:6-8 – I am praying to you because I know you will answer, O God. Bend down and listen as I pray. Show me your unfailing love in wonderful ways. By your mighty power you rescue those who seek refuge from their enemies. Guard me as you would guard your own eyes. Hide me in the shadow of your wings.

Psalm 18:1-3 – I love you, Lord; you are my strength. The Lord is my rock, my fortress and my savior. My God is my rock, in whom I find protection. He is my shield, the power that saves me and my place of safety. I called on the Lord, who is worthy of praise, and He saved me from my enemies.

Psalm 18:30-32 – God's way is perfect. All the Lord's promises prove true. He is a shield for all who look to Him for protection. For who is God except the Lord? God arms me with strength and He makes my way perfect.

Psalm 57:1 – Have mercy on me, O God, have mercy! I look to you for protection. I will hide beneath the shadow of your wings until the danger passes by.

Psalm 61:-4 – O God, listen to my cry! Hear my prayer! From the ends of the earth, I cry to you for help when my heart is overwhelmed. Lead me to the towering rock of safety, for you are my safe refuge, a fortress where my enemies cannot reach me. Let me live forever in your sanctuary, safe beneath the shelter of your wings!

When my mom was in her nineties she said two things – the first was that she could not lie because she was getting close to going home to be with Jesus. The second was that when she did get up there with Jesus she was going to run and dance with Him. Both of my mother's hips were bad. For years she had trouble walking. When she was younger and working, her co-workers called her speedy Gonzales. I inherited that from my mother too – I walk very fast – everywhere. I know she is in heaven with Jesus dancing and running at this very moment. God has her under his wings. He is our protector.

Isaiah 40:28 – Have you never heard? Have you never understood? The Lord is the everlasting God, the Creator of all the earth. He never grows weak or weary. No one can measure the depths of his understanding.

He gives power to the weak and strength to the powerless. Even youths will become weak and tired, and young men will fall in exhaustion. But those who trust in the Lord will find new strength. They will soar high on wings like eagles. They will run and not grow weary. They will walk and not faint.

Ruth 2:12 – May the Lord, the God of Israel, under whose wings you have come to take refuge, reward you fully for what you have done.

Numbers 6:24 – May the Lord bless you and protect you.

1 Samuel 2:9 – He will protect this faithful ones, but the wicked will disappear in darkness. No one will succeed by strength alone.

Psalm 5:12 – For you bless the godly, O Lord; you surround them with your shield of love.

2 Samuel 22:31 – God's way is perfect. All the Lord's promises prove true. He is a shield for all who look to him for protection.

Isaiah 33:21 – The Lord will be our Mighty One. He will be like a wide river of protection that no enemy can cross, that no enemy ship can sail upon.

CHAPTER 8
A Lifetime of Hope

Nette & Dickie
Our Other Mom & Dad

Just Who Is In Control?

Just to make sure you did not miss this earlier, it is important to know who is in control of everything – that is God. It is not a bad thing. Read on…

I cannot tell you how many times I asked my mom that question. If God is so good and loving, why is there is so much sadness, murder, depression, sickness. What a crappy world we live in. She kept telling me that God was in control. I kept asking if God was asleep. I mean, what was I supposed to think? It's rough out there.

But then I read that God often uses the devil as an instrument to advance the cause of God. The only power that the devil has is what God permits him to have. So whatever bad thing that happens, I cannot question. I do not know God's thoughts or plans. I can be assured that whatever happens is for a reason and that it will somehow glorify God.

1 John 4:4 – God's Spirit, who is in you, is greater than the devil, who is in the world.

1 Corinthians 10:13 – No test or temptation that comes your way is beyond the course of what others have had to face. All you need to remember is that God will never let you down; he will never let you be pushed past your limit; he will always be there to help you come through it.

Genesis 50:20 – You meant evil against me, but God meant it for good.

1 Peter 3:22 – Jesus has gone into heaven and is at God's right side ruling over angels, authorities, and powers.

Psalm 11:4 – But the Lord is in His holy temple. The Lord still rules from heaven. He watches everyone closely, examining every person on earth.

Philippians 3:21 – He will take our weak mortal bodies and change them into glorious bodies like his own, using the same power with which he will bring everything under his control.

Job 37:15 – Do you know how God controls the storm and causes the lightning to flash from his clouds?

Job 23:14 – So he will do to me whatever he has planned. He controls my destiny.

Daniel 2:21 – He controls the course of world events; he removed kings and sets up other kings. He gives wisdom to the wise and knowledge to the scholars.

2 Corinthians 5:14 – Either way, Christ's love controls us. Since we believe that Christ died for all, we also believe that we have all died to our old life.

Our God Loves Us & He Will Lead Us

I can't help myself, I just have to keep saying how awesome God is and how much He loves us. Trust Him and praise Him – there is nobody like Him. If we put our faith in Him, He will show us the right path. Even if we mess up, He is always there to catch us and help us.

Psalm 25:4-6 – Show me the right path, O Lord; point out the road for me to follow. Lead me by your truth and teach me, for you are the God who saves me. All day long I put my hope in you. Remember, O Lord, your compassion and unfailing love, which you have shown from long ages past.

Psalm 25:8-10 – The Lord is good and does what is right; he shows the proper path to those who go astray. He leads the humble in doing right, teaching them his way. The Lord leads with unfailing love and faithfulness all who keep his covenant and obey his demands.

This world is so corrupt, evil and violent. Sometimes it seems hopeless. But, there is always hope when we trust God.

Psalm 27:11-14 – Teach me how to live, O Lord. Lead me along the right path, for my enemies are waiting for me. Do not let me fall into their hands. For they accuse me of things I've never done; with every breath they threaten me with violence. Yet I am confident I will see the Lord's goodness while I am here in the land of the living. Wait patiently for the Lord. Be brave and courageous. Yes, wait patiently for the Lord.

The Devil Does Not Win

Okay, I am going to spoil the ending for anyone who has not yet read the Bible. The devil and his evil minions do not win. God wins! No person, no being, no angel, nothing compares to God. God is above everything.

Revelation 20:10 – Then the devil, who had deceived them, was thrown into the fiery lake of burning sulfur, joining the beast and the false prophet. There they will be tormented day and night forever and ever.

The devil and his minions are so mean and on the loose trying to hurt as many people as they can – trying to make them join the evil ones and stay away from God. The devil is such a jerk. The devil causes fear and confusion.

2 Timothy 1:7 – For God has not given us the spirit of fear, but of power, and of love, and of a sound mind.

1 Corinthians 14:33 – God is not the author of confusion.

Those people that do not accept God and that stand by the devil and his evil ways will pay with their lives. They are doomed. Sad, but true. There is still time for them to turn from their wicked ways. God is waiting. Pray for them.

Nahum 1:3-4 – The Lord is slow to get angry, but his power is great, and he never lets the guilty go unpunished. He displays his power in the whirlwind and the storm. The billowing clouds are the dust beneath his feet.

As I am writing this, the devil is trying to stop me. I know it. He is trying to put doubts in my mind making me relive some of the mistakes I made in the past. Thank you God for getting my mind clear every time I start to doubt. I am keeping my focus on God. God is in control.

Although it seems like the devil wins, he really doesn't. So, remember what my mother said to me….. Repeat it with me now…..

The Devil Can't Have Me No Matter What, I'll Hit Him In The Head and I'll Kick Him In The Butt……

Let's Talk Death

Up until the time my mom passed away, I was anxious, crying a lot, did not know how I was going to handle not having her. I knew it was coming. I was never without my mom. She lived with my husband and I when we got married. I lived with my mom and dad before I got married. She was my everything.

But after she passed away (in our house), something strange happened. That same day, the power went off suddenly and Kerry said it was my mom. She was still with us. Then something else happened about a month or so later. I was at peace with her death. I knew where she was – with Jesus.

She said she would find a way to come back to me. I was looking for her ghostly form. It is a spirit filled world after all. But she gave me something greater. She magnified my love for God and then God did the rest. I believe the Holy Spirit is helping me learn, helping me write this book to help others.

Getting back to death. We can cry and miss our loved ones. And it may seem like it will be forever until we see them again. But really it won't be that long. Just read below.....

1 Thessalonians 4:13 – We want you to be quite certain, brothers, about those who have died, to make sure that you do not grieve about them, like the other people who have no hope. I want you to know what happens to a Christian when he dies so that when it happens, you will not be full of sorrow, as those who have no hope.

For since we believe that Jesus died and then came back to life again, we can also believe that when Jesus returns, God will bring back with him all the Christians who have died.

So, let's recap. Here on this earth they had pain, they struggled, like we are still doing. In Heaven they have no pain, no struggles. My mom could hardly wait to go to Heaven so she could dance with Jesus. If I close my eyes, I can picture them dancing right now. We might not understand why God took them home at this time, but we must trust Him. God knew the right time to take them.

After all I have read, I truly believe that once the physical body dies, we (believers) go immediately into the presence of God. How can we be sad about that?

Philippians 1:21-23 – For to me, to live is Christ and to die is gain. If I am to go on living in the body, this will mean fruitful labor for me. Yet what shall I choose? I do not know. I am torn between the two: I desire to depart and be with Christ, which is better by far.

2 Corinthians 5:8 – We really want to be away from this body and be at home with the Lord.

What is hard for anyone to understand is why do some people die young? As I touched on earlier, my mom and dad went through this very thing. My brother, whom I never met since I was born fifteen or more years after he died, was young when he passed away. He got cancer. From what I am told it was a horrible thing to go through – not only for him, but for my parents and both my sisters (who were close in age to him). My mom told me that she clung to God. She knew God had his reasons.

My husband lost his father when he was young. His dad was young – only 50. His dad had a massive heart attack right in front of my husband. My husband had a hard time dealing with this sudden loss. I am so proud of Kerry, my husband, because he never lost his love for God. It was hard to lose someone he loved, but he knew God had a reason. I am sure we all have stories similar to these that we can relate to. Death is awful, but it's not the end.

Isaiah 57:1-2 – Good people pass away; the godly often die before their time. But no one seems to care or wonder why. No one seems to understand that God is protecting them from the evil to come. For those who follow godly paths will rest in peace when they die.

Romans 6:5-11 – Since we have been united with him in his death, we will also be raised to life as he was. We know that our old sinful selves were crucified with Christ so that sin might lose its power in our lives. We are no longer slaves to sin. For when we died with Christ we were set free from the power of sin. And since we died with Christ, we know we will also live with him. We are sure of this because Christ was raised from the dead and he will never die again. Death has no power over him. When he died, he died once to break the power of sin. But now that he lives, he lives for the glory of God. So you also should consider yourselves to be dead to the power of sin and alive to God through Jesus Christ.

The Resurrection of the Dead

Because of Jesus, the believers in Christ will rise from the dead when He comes back in His glory.

A new world, a new body, living with God for all eternity. A hope for everyone.

1 Corinthians 15:20-28

But in fact, Christ has been raised from the dead. He is the first of a great harvest of all who have died.

So you see, just as death came into the world through a man, now the resurrection from the dead has begun through another man. Just as everyone dies because we all belong to Adam, everyone who belongs to Christ will be given new life. But there is an order to this resurrection: Christ was raised as the first of the harvest; then all who belong to Christ will be raised when he comes back.

After that the end will come, when he will turn the Kingdom over to God the Father, having destroyed every ruler and authority and power. For Christ must reign until he humbles all his enemies beneath his feet. And the last enemy to be destroyed is death. For the Scriptures say, God has put all things under his authority. (Of course, when it says "all things are under his authority," that does not include God himself, who gave Christ his authority.)

Then, when all things are under his authority, the Son will put himself under God's authority, so that God, who gave his Son authority over all things, will be utterly supreme over everything everywhere.

1 Corinthians 15:35-58

But someone may ask, how will the dead be raised? What kind of bodies will they have? What a foolish question! When you put a seed into the ground, it doesn't grow into a plant unless it dies first. And what you put in the ground is not the plant that will grow, but only a bare seed of wheat or whatever you are planting. Then God gives it the new body he wants it to have. A different plant grows from each kind of seed. Similarly there are different kinds of flesh—one kind for humans, another for animals, another for birds, and another for fish.

There are also bodies in the heavens and bodies on the earth. The glory of the heavenly bodies is different from the glory of the earthly bodies. The sun has one kind of glory, while the moon and stars each have another kind. And even the stars differ from each other in their glory.

It is the same way with the resurrection of the dead. Our earthly bodies are planted in the ground when we die, but they will be raised to live forever. Our bodies are buried in brokenness, but they will be raised in glory. They are buried in weakness, but they will be raised in strength.

They are buried as natural human bodies, but they will be raised as spiritual bodies. For just as there are natural bodies, there are also spiritual bodies.

The Scriptures tell us, the first man, Adam, became a living person. But the last Adam—that is, Christ—is a life-giving Spirit. What comes first is the natural body, then the spiritual body comes later. Adam, the first man, was made from the dust of the earth, while Christ, the second man, came from heaven. Earthly people are like the earthly man, and heavenly people are like the heavenly man. Just as we are now like the earthly man, we will someday be like the heavenly man.

What I am saying, dear brothers and sisters, is that our physical bodies cannot inherit the Kingdom of God. These dying bodies cannot inherit what will last forever.

CHAPTER 9

Interesting Tidbits in the Bible

Kerry's Mom

God Always Keeps His Promises

I cannot tell you how many times someone has promised me something and it did not come true. After a while the word "promise" means nothing. If we are waiting on earthly promises, we will be disappointed.

God always keeps His promises. Remember the rainbow covenant.

Genesis 9:13-I have placed my rainbow in the cloud. It is the sign of my covenant with you and with all the earth. When I send clouds over the earth, the rainbow will appear in the clouds. When I see the rainbow in the clouds, I will remember the eternal covenant between God and every living creature on earth. Then God said to Noah – Yes, this rainbow is the sign of the covenant I am confirming with all the creatures on earth.

Psalm 12:6 – The Lord's promises are pure, like silver refined in a furnace, purified seven times over.

While we wait for our true place to live, God comforts us in all our trials and tribulations. He said He would always be there for us. We should also comfort others. This is a promise we should try to keep.

2 Corinthians 1:3-7 – All praise to God, the Father of our Lord Jesus Christ. God is our merciful Father and the source of all comfort.

He comforts us in all our troubles so that we can comfort others. When they are troubled, we will be able to give them the same comfort God has given us. For the more we suffer for Christ, the more God will shower us with his comfort through Christ.

Even when we are weighed down with troubles, it is for your comfort and salvation. For when we ourselves are comforted, we will certainly comfort you. Then you can patiently endure the same things we suffer. We are confident that as you share in our sufferings, you will also share in the comfort God gives us.

2 Samuel 22:31 – God's way is perfect. All the Lord's promises prove true. He is a shield for all who look to him for protection.

Numbers 23:19 – God is not a man, so he does not lie. He is not human, so he does not change his mind. Has he ever spoken and failed to act? Has he ever promised and not carried it through?

Remember this next time you see a beautiful rainbow.

Genesis 9:14 – When I send clouds over the earth, the rainbow will appear in the clouds.

Genesis 9:16 – When I see the rainbow in the clouds, I will remember the eternal covenant between God and every living creature on earth.

Genesis 9:17 – Then God said to Noah – Yes, this rainbow is the sign of the covenant I am confirming with all the creatures on earth.

The Ark of the Covenant

Okay, show of hands – who always watches any show that talks about the Ark of the Covenant? Read the plans below and then close your eyes and picture what this looked like – you will not be disappointed. All you individuals that want to be or are Archeologists read on….

Exodus 25:10-40

Have the people make an Ark of acacia wood—a sacred chest 45 inches long, 27 inches wide, and 27 inches high. Overlay it inside and outside with pure gold, and run a molding of gold all around it. Cast four gold rings and attach them to its four feet, two rings on each side. Make poles from acacia wood, and overlay them with gold. Insert the poles into the rings at the sides of the Ark to carry it. These carrying poles must stay inside the rings; never remove them. When the Ark is finished, place inside it the stone tablets inscribed with the terms of the covenant, which I will give to you.

Then make the Ark's cover—the place of atonement—from pure gold. It must be 45 inches long and 27 inches wide. Then make two cherubim from hammered gold, and place them on the two ends of the atonement cover. Mold the cherubim on each end of the atonement cover, making it all of one piece of gold. The cherubim will face each other and look down on the atonement cover. With their wings spread above it, they will protect it.

Place inside the Ark the stone tablets inscribed with the terms of the covenant, which I will give to you. Then put the atonement cover on top of the Ark. I will meet with you there and talk to you from above the atonement cover between the gold cherubim that hover over the Ark of the Covenant. From there I will give you my commands for the people of Israel.

The Table

Then make a table of acacia wood, 36 inches long, 18 inches wide, and 27 inches high. Overlay it with pure gold and run a gold molding around the edge. Decorate it with a 3-inch border all around, and run a gold molding along the border. Make four gold rings for the table and attach them at the four corners next to the four legs. Attach the rings near the border to hold the poles that are used to carry the table. Make these poles from acacia wood, and overlay them with gold. Make special containers of pure gold for the table— bowls, ladles, pitchers, and jars—to be used in pouring out liquid offerings. Place the Bread of the Presence on the table to remain before me at all times.

The Lampstand

Make a lampstand of pure, hammered gold. Make the entire lampstand and its decorations of one piece—the base, center stem, lamp cups, buds, and petals. Make it with six branches going out from the center stem, three on each side.

Each of the six branches will have three lamp cups shaped like almond blossoms, complete with buds and petals. Craft the center stem of the lampstand with four lamp cups shaped like almond blossoms, complete with buds and petals. There will also be an almond bud beneath each pair of branches where the six branches extend from the center stem.

The almond buds and branches must all be of one piece with the center stem, and they must be hammered from pure gold. Then make the seven lamps for the lampstand, and set them so they reflect their light forward.

The lamp snuffers and trays must also be made of pure gold. You will need 75 pounds of pure gold for the lampstand and its accessories. Be sure that you make everything according to the pattern I have shown you here on the mountain.

Can you picture this? Aren't you impressed?

What a glorious God we have! All praise, glory and honor to our Father.

We Can Always Rely On God

God is our strength and we can always rely on Him. There is no power on earth or in the heavens that is like God. Remember, He is in control and will always look out for His people – all those who believe in Him.

Psalm 18:1-3 – I love you, Lord; you are my strength. The Lord is my rock, my fortress, and my savior; my God is my rock, in whom I find protection. He is my shield, the power that saves me and my place of safety. I called on the Lord, who is worthy of praise and he saved me from my enemies.

Just listen to the power of God. I do not ever want Him mad at me. Thank you God for always being there for us and always looking out for us. If the below description does not make you want to fall to your knees and praise Him, I don't know what will.

Psalm 18:7-15 – Then the earth quaked and trembled. The foundations of the mountains shook; they quaked because of his anger. Smoke poured from his nostrils; fierce flames leaped from his mouth. Glowing coals blazed forth from him. He opened the heavens and came down; dark storm clouds were beneath his feet. Mounted on a mighty angelic being, he flew, soaring on the wings of the wind. He shrouded himself in darkness, veiling his approach with dark rain clouds.

Thick clouds shielded the brightness around him and rained down hail and burning coals. The Lord thundered from heaven; the voice of the Most High resounded amid the hail and burning coals. He shot his arrows and scattered his enemies; great bolts of lightning flashed and they were confused.

Then at your command, O Lord, at the blast of your breath, the bottom of the sea could be seen, and the foundations of the earth were laid to bare.

Remember those verses next time there is a thunder and lightning storm, or heavy rain, or hail. And to see the bottom of the sea – unbelievable.

Always rely on our Lord who loves us more than anything.

Psalm 33:18 – But the Lord watches over those who fear him, those who rely on his unfailing love.

Isaiah 50:10 – Who among you fears the Lord and obeys his servant? If you are walking in darkness, without a ray of light, trust in the Lord and rely on your God.

Job 37:5 – God's voice is glorious in the thunder. We can't even imagine the greatness of his power.

We Have Everlasting Hope

Jesus is our everlasting hope. All these problems we now have will be nothing when Jesus comes back to rule. So stay on the right track so we can be with Him for eternity.

Isaiah 9:2 – The people who walk in darkness will see a great light. For those who live in a land of deep darkness, a light will shine.

Isaiah 9:6-7 – For a child is born to us, a son is given to us. The government will rest on his shoulders. And he will be called – Wonderful Counselor, Mighty God, Everlasting Father, Prince of Peace. His government and its peace will never end. He will rule with fairness and justice from the throne of his ancestor David for all eternity. The passionate commitment of the Lord of Heaven's armies will make this happen.

Read about the Highway of Holiness – a place with no dangers.

Isaiah 35:8-10 – And a great road will go through that once deserted land. It will be named the Highway of Holiness. Evil minded people will never travel on it. It will be only for those who walk in God's ways; fools will never walk there. Lions will not lurk along its course, nor any other ferocious beasts. There will be no other dangers. Only the redeemed will walk on it. Those who have been ransomed by the Lord will return. They will enter Jerusalem singing, crowed with everlasting joy. Sorrow and mourning will disappear, and they will be filled with joy and gladness.

Ezekiel – A Fascinating Chapter in the Bible

Ezekiel has some of the most descriptive, fascinating verses in the Bible. Just start with Ezekiel 1. I could not even begin to describe this to you. You just have to read it.

A Vision of Living Beings

Ezekiel 1:4-28 –

As I looked, I saw a great storm coming from the north, driving before it a huge cloud that flashed with lightning and shone with brilliant light. There was fire inside the cloud, and in the middle of the fire glowed something like gleaming amber. From the center of the cloud came four living beings that looked human, except that each had four faces and four wings. Their legs were straight, and their feet had hooves like those of a calf and shone like burnished bronze. Under each of their four wings I could see human hands. So each of the four beings had four faces and four wings. The wings of each living being touched the wings of the beings beside it. Each one moved straight forward in any direction without turning around.

Each had a human face in the front, the face of a lion on the right side, the face of an ox on the left side, and the face of an eagle at the back. Each had two pairs of outstretched wings—one pair stretched out to touch the wings of the living beings on either side of it, and the other pair covered its body.

They went in whatever direction the spirit chose, and they moved straight forward in any direction without turning around.

The living beings looked like bright coals of fire or brilliant torches, and lightning seemed to flash back and forth among them. And the living beings darted to and fro like flashes of lightning.

As I looked at these beings, I saw four wheels touching the ground beside them, one wheel belonging to each. The wheels sparkled as if made of beryl. All four wheels looked alike and were made the same; each wheel had a second wheel turning crosswise within it. The beings could move in any of the four directions they faced, without turning as they moved. The rims of the four wheels were tall and frightening, and they were covered with eyes all around.

When the living beings moved, the wheels moved with them. When they flew upward, the wheels went up, too. The spirit of the living beings was in the wheels. So wherever the spirit went, the wheels and the living beings also went. When the beings moved, the wheels moved. When the beings stopped, the wheels stopped. When the beings flew upward, the wheels rose up, for the spirit of the living beings was in the wheels.

Spread out above them was a surface like the sky, glittering like crystal. Beneath this surface the wings of each living being stretched out to touch the others' wings, and each had two wings covering its body.

As they flew, their wings sounded to me like waves crashing against the shore or like the voice of the Almighty or like the shouting of a mighty army. When they stopped, they let down their wings. As they stood with wings lowered, a voice spoke from beyond the crystal surface above them.

Above this surface was something that looked like a throne made of blue lapis lazuli. And on this throne high above was a figure whose appearance resembled a man. From what appeared to be his waist up, he looked like gleaming amber, flickering like a fire. And from his waist down, he looked like a burning flame, shining with splendor. All around him was a glowing halo, like a rainbow shining in the clouds on a rainy day. This is what the glory of the LORD looked like to me. When I saw it, I fell face down on the ground, and I heard someone's voice speaking to me.

Wasn't that one of the most exciting things you have ever read?

The power of God is unimaginable and breathtaking.

Job 37:5 – God's voice is glorious in the thunder. We can't even imagine the greatness of his power.

CHAPTER 10

The Comforting Chapter

*Our Beautiful Tree
God's Creation*

Being Judged

This used to scare me. Holy moly, with all the sins I have committed, we will be there for days while the Lord reads and reviews them. I worried that I would never be allowed in. Stopped at the gate by a huge angel bouncer.

Matthew 12:36 – On the day of judgement, men will render account for every careless word they utter.

Romans 14:10, 12 – The Lord will judge his people. For we will all stand before God's judgement seat…so then each of us will give an account of himself to God.

But then I read….

Romans 8:1 – Therefore there is now no condemnation for those who are in Christ Jesus.

Whew. So, if I am reading this right, because Jesus died for us (and forgave our sins) and since we believe and love God (and for the most part lived in faith and trust), our sins are already forgiven.

I am guessing, and hope I am right, that we will have our sins read but we have already been pardoned by Jesus. What a relief. Thank you Jesus. Through God's Grace we are forgiven. Again, all praise, glory and honor to you almighty God forever and ever.

1 John 2:12 – I am writing to you who are God's children because your sins have been forgiven through Jesus.

Hebrews 10:10 – For God's will was for us to be made holy by the sacrifice of the body of Jesus Christ, once for all time.

1 Corinthians 11:32 – Yet when we are judged by the Lord, we are being disciplined so that we will not be condemned along with the world.

Romans 5:6 – When we were utterly helpless, Christ came at just the right time and died for us sinners.

2 Corinthians 5:1 – Either way, Christ's love controls us. Since we believe that Christ died for all, we also believe that we have all died to our old life.

1 Peter 3:18 – Christ suffered for our sins once for all time. He never sinned, but he died for sinners to bring you safely home to God. He suffered physical death, but he was raised to life in the Spirit.

The Holy Spirit – Our Comforter

My mom always said to rely on the invisible hands of God. The Holy Spirit is our helper, comforter, and to me, His invisible hands are always there to help us get up if we fall. Remember the Holy Trinity – the Father, the Son, and the Holy Spirit.

Acts 2:1-4 – On the day of Pentecost all the believers were meeting together in one place. Suddenly there was a sound from heaven like the roaring of a mighty windstorm and it filled the house where they were meeting. Then, what looked like flames or tongues of fire appeared and settled on each of them. And everyone present was filled with the Holy Spirit and began speaking in other languages, as the Holy Spirit has this ability.

Romans 5:3-5 – We can rejoice too, when we run into problems and trials, for we know that they help us develop endurance. And endurance develops strength of character, and character strengthens our confident hope of salvation. And this hope will not lead to disappointment. For we know how dearly God loves us, because he has given us the Holy Spirit to fill our hearts with his love.

Because the Holy Spirit was sent to help us, we should let Him guide our lives.

Galatians 5:16-18 – So I say, let the Holy Spirit guide your lives. Then you won't be doing what your sinful nature craves.

The sinful nature wants to do evil, which is just the opposite of what the Spirit wants. And the Spirit gives us desires that are the opposite of what the sinful nature wants. These two forces are constantly fighting each other, so you are not free to carry out your good intentions. But when you are directed by the Spirit, you are not under obligation to the law of Moses.

Galatians 5:22-23 – But the Holy Spirit produces this kind of fruit in our lives: love, joy, peace, patience, kindness, goodness, faithfulness, gentleness and self-control. There is no law against these things.

1 Corinthians 2:10-12 – But it was to us that God revealed these things by his Spirit. For his Spirit searches out everything and shows us God's deep secrets. No one can know a person's thoughts except that person's own spirt, and no one can know God's thoughts except God's own Spirit. And we have received God's Spirit (not the world's spirit), so we can know the wonderful things God has freely given us.

The Holy Spirit gives us spiritual gifts.

1 Corinthians 12:4-11 – There are different kinds of spiritual gifts, but the same Spirit is the source of them all. There are different kinds of service, but we serve the same Lord. God works in different ways, but it is the same God who does the work in all of us.

A spiritual gift is given to each of us so we can help each other. To one person the Spirit gives the ability to give wise advice; to another the same Spirit gives a message of special knowledge.

The same Spirit gives great faith to another, and to someone else the one Spirit gives the gift of healing. He gives one person the power to perform miracles, and another the ability to prophesy.

He gives someone else the ability to discern whether a message is from the Spirit of God or from another spirit. Still another person is given the ability to speak in unknown languages, while another is given the ability to interpret what is being said.

It is the one and only Spirit who distributes all these gifts. He alone decides which gift each person should have.

John 14:26 – But when the Father sends the Advocate as my representative – that is, the Holy Spirit – he will teach you everything and will remind you of everything I have told you.

Luke 24:49 – And now I will send the Holy Spirit, just as my Father promised. But stay here in the city until the Holy Spirit comes and fills you with power from heaven.

Let's Talk About Spiritual Blessings

I cannot state it enough – God loves us so much that He gives us so much. A place to live with Him, a Savior to lead us and love us, and spiritual blessings.

Ephesians 1:3-14

All praise to God, the Father of our Lord Jesus Christ, who has blessed us with every spiritual blessing in the heavenly realms because we are united with Christ. Even before he made the world, God loved us and chose us in Christ to be holy and without fault in his eyes. God decided in advance to adopt us into his own family by bringing us to himself through Jesus Christ. This is what he wanted to do, and it gave him great pleasure. So we praise God for the glorious grace he has poured out on us who belong to his dear Son. He is so rich in kindness and grace that he purchased our freedom with the blood of his Son and forgave our sins. He has showered his kindness on us, along with all wisdom and understanding.

God has now revealed to us his mysterious will regarding Christ—which is to fulfill his own good plan. And this is the plan: At the right time he will bring everything together under the authority of Christ—everything in heaven and on earth. Furthermore, because we are united with Christ, we have received an inheritance from God, for he chose us in advance, and he makes everything work out according to his plan.

God's purpose was that we Jews who were the first to trust in Christ would bring praise and glory to God. And now you Gentiles have also heard the truth, the Good News that God saves you. And when you believed in Christ, he identified you as his own by giving you the Holy Spirit, whom he promised long ago. The Spirit is God's guarantee that he will give us the inheritance he promised and that he has purchased us to be his own people. He did this so we would praise and glorify him.

Not only do we get blessings, but read about the crowns available to us.

Psalm 149:4 – For the Lord delights in his people; he crowns the humble with victory.

Isaiah 62:3 – The Lord will hold you in his hand for all to see – a splendid crown in the hand of God.

Zechariah 9:16 – On that day the Lord their God will rescue his people, just as a shepherd rescues his sheep. They will sparkle in his land like jewels in a crown.

Psalm 103:4 – He redeems me from death and crowns me with love and tender mercies.

The Armor Of God

I have the below scripture on my desk at work. This really helps me keep my focus on God and helps me face any challenges or trials at work. If nothing else, try to write this down and keep it with you. It will really help you. Remember, the devil and his evil minions are hard at work trying to bring you down and away from God. Do not let him win.

Put on your armor..

Ephesians 6:10-19

A final word: Be strong in the Lord and in his mighty power. Put on all of God's armor so that you will be able to stand firm against all strategies of the devil. For we are not fighting against flesh-and-blood enemies, but against evil rulers and authorities of the unseen world, against mighty powers in this dark world, and against evil spirits in the heavenly places.

Therefore, put on every piece of God's armor so you will be able to resist the enemy in the time of evil. Then after the battle you will still be standing firm. Stand your ground, putting on the belt of truth and the body armor of God's righteousness. For shoes, put on the peace that comes from the Good News so that you will be fully prepared. In addition to all of these, hold up the shield of faith to stop the fiery arrows of the devil. Put on salvation as your helmet, and take the sword of the Spirit, which is the word of God.

Pray in the Spirit at all times and on every occasion. Stay alert and be persistent in your prayers for all believers everywhere.

And pray for me, too. Ask God to give me the right words so I can boldly explain God's mysterious plan that the Good News is for Jews and Gentiles alike. I am in chains now, still preaching this message as God's ambassador. So pray that I will keep on speaking boldly for him, as I should.

A few more verses about the Armor of God –

1 Thessalonians 5:8 – But let us who live in the light be clearheaded, protected by the armor of faith and love, and wearing our helmet the confidence of our salvation.

Psalm 91:4 – He will cover you with his feathers. He will shelter you with his wings. His faithful promises are your armor and protection.

Jesus Is Our Everything

In the next verses from Colossians 1:15-23, there is so much hope. Being a writer, I loved the first sentence – "Christ is the visible image of the invisible God". Read it for yourself and see what I mean. This whole Scripture is so powerful.

Colossians 1-15:23 – Christ is the visible image of the invisible God. He existed before anything was created and is supreme over all creation, for through him God created everything in the heavenly realms and on earth.

He made the things we can see and the things we cannot see, such as thrones, kingdoms, rulers, and authorities in the unseen world. Everything was created through him and for him.

He existed before anything else, and he holds all creation together. Christ is also the head of the church, which is his body. He is the beginning, supreme over all who rise from the dead. So he is first in everything.

For God in all his fullness was pleased to live in Christ, and through him God reconciled everything to himself. He made peace with everything in heaven and on earth by means of Christ's blood on the cross.

This includes you who were once far away from God. You were his enemies, separated from him by your evil thoughts and actions. Yet now he has reconciled you to himself through the death of Christ in his physical body.

As a result, he has brought you into his own presence, and you are holy and blameless as you stand before him without a single fault.

But you must continue to believe this truth and stand firmly in it. Don't drift away from the assurance you received when you heard the Good News. The Good News has been preached all over the world and, I, Paul, have been appointed as God's servant to proclaim it.

A few more verses about our "invisible" but all knowing and ever present God.

Romans 1:20 – For ever since the world was created, people have seen the earth and sky. Through everything God made, they can clearly see his invisible qualities – his eternal power and divine nature. So they have no excuse for not knowing God.

Hebrews 11:27 – It was by faith that Moses left the land of Egypt, not fearing the king's anger. He kept right on going because he kept his eyes on the one who is invisible.

CHAPTER 11

The Return of Jesus

Baby – Our Lop

Our New Bodies

We will get new bodies when Christ comes back. I am sure we will know each other – but isn't it great to know that these broken down bodies will be replaced with perfect bodies made by God Himself.

2 Corinthians 5:1-5 – For we know that when this earthly tent we live in is taken down (that is, when we die and leave this earthly body), we will have a house in heaven, an eternal body made for us by God himself and not by human hands. We grow weary in our present bodies, and we long to put on our heavenly bodies like new clothing. For we will put on heavenly bodies; we will not be spirits without bodies. While we live in these earthly bodies, we groan and sigh, but it's not that we want to die and get rid of these bodies that clothe us. Rather, we want to put on our new bodies so that these dying bodies will be swallowed up by life. God himself has prepared us for this, and as a guarantee he has given us his Holy Spirit.

Remember when Jesus rose from the dead.

Luke 24:35-40 – Then the two from Emmaus told their story of how Jesus had appeared to them as they were walking along the road, and how they had recognized him as he was breaking the bread. And just as they were telling about it, Jesus himself was suddenly standing there among them. Peace be with you, he said.

But the whole group was startled and frightened, thinking they were seeing a ghost. Why are you frightened? he asked. Why are your hearts filled with doubt? Look at my hands. Look at my feet. You can see that it's really me. Touch me and make sure that I am not a ghost, because ghosts don't have bodies, as you see that I do.

Romans 8:23 – And we believers also groan, even though we have the Holy Spirit within us as a foretaste of future glory, for we long for our bodies to be released from sin and suffering. We, too, wait with eager hope for the day when God will give us our full rights as his adopted children, including the new bodies he has promised us.

I have included on the next few pages 1 Chronicles 15 in its entirety. This talks further about our new bodies.

I believe the following scripture is so powerful, that nothing else needs to be said – just read on. Here it is in its entirety.

1 Corinthians 15

The Resurrection of Christ

Let me now remind you, dear brothers and sisters, of the Good News I preached to you before. You welcomed it then, and you still stand firm in it. It is this Good News that saves you if you continue to believe the message I told you—unless, of course, you believed something that was never true in the first place.

I passed on to you what was most important and what had also been passed on to me. Christ died for our sins, just as the Scriptures said. He was buried, and he was raised from the dead on the third day, just as the Scriptures said. He was seen by Peter and then by the Twelve. After that, he was seen by more than 500 of his followers at one time, most of whom are still alive, though some have died. Then he was seen by James and later by all the apostles. Last of all, as though I had been born at the wrong time, I also saw him. For I am the least of all the apostles. In fact, I'm not even worthy to be called an apostle after the way I persecuted God's church.

But whatever I am now, it is all because God poured out his special favor on me—and not without results. For I have worked harder than any of the other apostles; yet it was not I but God who was working through me by his grace.

So it makes no difference whether I preach or they preach, for we all preach the same message you have already believed.

The Resurrection of the Dead

But tell me this—since we preach that Christ rose from the dead, why are some of you saying there will be no resurrection of the dead? For if there is no resurrection of the dead, then Christ has not been raised either. And if Christ has not been raised, then all our preaching is useless, and your faith is useless. And we apostles would all be lying about God—for we have said that God raised Christ from the grave. But that can't be true if there is no resurrection of the dead.

And if there is no resurrection of the dead, then Christ has not been raised. And if Christ has not been raised, then your faith is useless and you are still guilty of your sins.

In that case, all who have died believing in Christ are lost! And if our hope in Christ is only for this life, we are more to be pitied than anyone in the world.

But in fact, Christ has been raised from the dead. He is the first of a great harvest of all who have died. So you see, just as death came into the world through a man, now the resurrection from the dead has begun through another man. Just as everyone dies because we all belong to Adam, everyone who belongs to Christ will be given new life.

But there is an order to this resurrection: Christ was raised as the first of the harvest; then all who belong to Christ will be raised when he comes back.

After that the end will come, when he will turn the Kingdom over to God the Father, having destroyed every ruler and authority and power. For Christ must reign until he humbles all his enemies beneath his feet. And the last enemy to be destroyed is death. For the Scriptures say, God has put all things under his authority. (Of course, when it says "all things are under his authority," that does not include God himself, who gave Christ his authority.) Then, when all things are under his authority, the Son will put himself under God's authority, so that God, who gave his Son authority over all things, will be utterly supreme over everything everywhere.

If the dead will not be raised, what point is there in people being baptized for those who are dead? Why do it unless the dead will someday rise again? And why should we ourselves risk our lives hour by hour? For I swear, dear brothers and sisters, that I face death daily. This is as certain as my pride in what Christ Jesus our Lord has done in you. And what value was there in fighting wild beasts—those people of Ephesus, if there will be no resurrection from the dead? And if there is no resurrection, let's feast and drink, for tomorrow we die! Don't be fooled by those who say such things, for bad company corrupts good character.

Think carefully about what is right, and stop sinning. For to your shame I say that some of you don't know God at all.

The Resurrection Body

But someone may ask, how will the dead be raised? What kind of bodies will they have? What a foolish question! When you put a seed into the ground, it doesn't grow into a plant unless it dies first. And what you put in the ground is not the plant that will grow, but only a bare seed of wheat or whatever you are planting.

Then God gives it the new body he wants it to have. A different plant grows from each kind of seed. Similarly there are different kinds of flesh—one kind for humans, another for animals, another for birds, and another for fish.

There are also bodies in the heavens and bodies on the earth. The glory of the heavenly bodies is different from the glory of the earthly bodies. The sun has one kind of glory, while the moon and stars each have another kind. And even the stars differ from each other in their glory.

It is the same way with the resurrection of the dead. Our earthly bodies are planted in the ground when we die, but they will be raised to live forever. Our bodies are buried in brokenness, but they will be raised in glory. They are buried in weakness, but they will be raised in strength.

They are buried as natural human bodies, but they will be raised as spiritual bodies. For just as there are natural bodies, there are also spiritual bodies.

The Scriptures tell us, the first man, Adam, became a living person. But the last Adam—that is, Christ—is a life-giving Spirit. What comes first is the natural body, then the spiritual body comes later. Adam, the first man, was made from the dust of the earth, while Christ, the second man, came from heaven. Earthly people are like the earthly man, and heavenly people are like the heavenly man. Just as we are now like the earthly man, we will someday be like the heavenly man.

What I am saying, dear brothers and sisters, is that our physical bodies cannot inherit the Kingdom of God. These dying bodies cannot inherit what will last forever.

But let me reveal to you a wonderful secret. We will not all die, but we will all be transformed! It will happen in a moment, in the blink of an eye, when the last trumpet is blown. For when the trumpet sounds, those who have died will be raised to live forever. And we who are living will also be transformed.

For our dying bodies must be transformed into bodies that will never die; our mortal bodies must be transformed into immortal bodies.

Then, when our dying bodies have been transformed into bodies that will never die, this Scripture will be fulfilled: Death is swallowed up in victory. O death, where is your victory? O death, where is your sting?

For sin is the sting that results in death, and the law gives sin its power. But thank God! He gives us victory over sin and death through our Lord Jesus Christ. So, my dear brothers and sisters, be strong and immovable. Always work enthusiastically for the Lord, for you know that nothing you do for the Lord is ever useless.

The Last Days

You do not want to wait for the last minute to believe in God, confess your sins, and be saved. Do it now. We do not know the time that Jesus will come back. You do not want to be caught in something that you won't be able to get out of – get right with God now.

Read the below passages from 2 Timothy and tell me this does not sound like the current world we live in.

2 Timothy 3:1-5 – You should know this, Timothy, that in the last days there will be very difficult times. For people will love only themselves and their money. They will be boastful and proud, scoffing at God, disobedient to their parents and ungrateful. They will consider nothing sacred.

They will be unloving and unforgiving; they will slander others and have no self-control. They will be cruel and hate what is good. They will betray their friends, be reckless, be puffed up with pride, and love pleasure rather than God. They will act religious, but they will reject the power that could make them godly. Stay away from people like that.

The Rapture

The rapture is something my mom and I looked forward to – and we still do. It is going to be something else. I cannot even begin to describe it. Check it out…

1 Thessalonians 4:16-17- For the Lord Himself will come down from heaven with a commanding shout, with the voice of the archangel, and with the trumpet call of God. First, the believers who have died will rise from their graves. Then, together with them, we who are still alive and remain on the earth will be caught up in the clouds to meet the Lord in the air. Then we will be with the Lord forever.

1 Corinthians 15:50-54 – What I am saying, dear brothers and sisters, is that our physical bodies cannot inherit the Kingdom of God. These dying bodies cannot inherit what will last forever.

But let me reveal to you a wonderful secret. We will not all die, but we will all be transformed. It will happen in a moment, in the blink of an eye, when the last trumpet is blown. For when the trumpet sounds, those who have died will be raised to live forever. And we who are living will also be transformed. For our dying bodies must be transformed into bodies that will never die; our mortal bodies must be transformed into immortal bodies.

Then, when our dying bodies have been transformed into bodies that will never die, this Scripture will be fulfilled – death is swallowed up in victory.

John 11:25 – Jesus told her, I am the resurrection and the life. Anyone who believes in me will live, even after dying.

Jesus has come down from Heaven for us.

Philippians 1:6 – And I am certain that God, who began the good work within you, will continue his work until it is finally finished on the day when Christ Jesus returns.

1 Corinthians 1:8 - He will keep you strong to the end so that you will be free from all blame on the day when our Lord Jesus Christ returns.

John 3:13 – No one has ever gone to heaven and returned. But the Son of Man has come down from heaven.

John 6:33 – The true bread of God is the one who comes down from heaven and gives life to the world.

John 6:38 – For I have come down from heaven to do the will of God who sent me, not to do my own will.

Revelation – A Must Read For Everyone

As I stated earlier, mom and my favorite book in the Bible is Revelation. We have been looking forward to the rapture for years. Since I do not want to add or take anything away from the book of Revelation, I am going to include quotes from the Bible. I will include my little notes of interesting things that I have learned along the way. But really, I encourage everyone to read Revelation. It really is amazing and life changing.

God promises a blessing to all who read Revelation. I don't know about you, but I need all the blessings I can get.

I do not want to add or take anything away from Revelation. So I will provide verses below. There are so many more that can help you, but the below ones are some of my favorites.

Revelation 1:1-3 –This is a revelation from Jesus Christ, which God gave him to show his servants the events that must soon take place. He sent an angel to present this revelation to his servant John, who faithfully reported everything he saw. This is his report of the word of God and the testimony of Jesus Christ.

God blesses the one who reads the words of this prophecy to the church, and he blesses all who listen to its message and obey what it says, for the time is near.

Revelation is the revealing of Jesus Christ. We will learn that as King of kings and Lord of lords, Jesus will rule over His unending Kingdom on earth. Wow – unending Kingdom with Jesus. I can hardly wait.

The Holy Spirit will teach us the truth and open our understanding of the Word of God –

John 16:13 – When the Spirit of truth comes, he will guide you into all truth. He will not speak on his own but will tell you what he has heard. He will tell you about the future.

<u>The Return of Jesus</u>

Revelation 1:7 – Look! He comes with the clouds of heaven. And everyone will see Him – even those who pierced Him. And all the nations of the world will mourn for Him. Yes ! Amen!

Revelation 1:8 – I am Alpha and Omega, the beginning and the ending, said the Lord, which is and which was and which is to come, the Almighty.

Everyone gets to see Jesus – I know I don't feel worthy, but I am excited even now just thinking about it.

Revelation 1:18 – I am the living one. I died, but look – I am alive forever and even hold the keys of death and the grave.

He That Has An Ear – Please Listen

In the Seven Churches (Ephesus, Smyrna, Pergamum, Thyatira, Sardis, Philadelphia, Laodicea), I found the below important for everyone to read.

All of Revelation is important and should be read. From Genesis to Revelation, each book of the Bible gives us hope and tells of our future home with God, our Father, the Son, and the Holy Spirit.

To Ephesus –

Revelation 2:7 –Anyone with ears to hear must listen to the Spirit and understand what he is saying to the churches. To everyone who is victorious I will give fruit from the tree of life in the paradise of God.

To Smyrna –

Revelation 2:11 – Anyone with ears to hear must listen to the Spirit and understand what he is saying to the churches. Whoever is victorious will not be harmed by the second death.

To Pergamum –

Revelation 2:17 – Anyone with ears to hear must listen to the Spirit and understand what he is saying to the churches. To everyone who is victorious I will give some of the manna that has been hidden away in heaven. And I will give to each one a white stone, and on the stone will be engraved a new name that no one understands except the one who receives it.

To Thyatira –

Revelation 2:26 – To all who are victorious, who obey me to the very end, to them I will give authority over all the nations.

Revelation 2:29 – Anyone with ears to hear must listen to the Spirit and understand what he is saying to the churches.

To Sardis –

Revelation 3:5-6 – All who are victorious will be clothed in white. I will never erase their names from the Book of Life, but I will announce before my Father and his angels that they are mine. Anyone with ears to hear must listen to the Spirit and understand what he is saying to the churches.

To Philadelphia –

Revelation 3:12-13 – All who are victorious will become pillars in the Temple of my God, and they will never have to leave it. And I will write on them the name of my God, and they will be citizens in the city of my God – the new Jerusalem that comes down from heaven from my God. And I will also write on them my new name. Anyone with ears to hear must listen to the Spirit and understand what he is saying to the churches.

To Laodicea –

Revelation 3:20-22 – Look! I stand at the door and knock. If you hear my voice and open the door, I will come in and we will share a meal together as friends. Those who are victorious will sit with me on my throne, just as I was victorious and sat with my Father on his throne.

Anyone with ears to hear must listen to the Spirit and understand what he is saying to the churches.

Reading the next verses make me want to get on my knees and worship before God. What a sight to behold. Without the loving and forgiving Grace of God, we are doomed – if we don't believe, have faith and trust in the Father, Son, and the Holy Spirit.

Revelation 4:2-6 – Then as I looked, I saw a door standing open in heaven and the same voice I had heard before spoke to me like a trumpet blast. The voice said, Come up here and I will show you what must happen after this. And instantly I was in the Spirit and I saw a throne in heaven and someone sitting on it.

The one sitting on the throne was as brilliant as gemstones – like jasper and carnelian. And the glow of an emerald circled his throne like a rainbow. Twenty-four thrones surrounded him and twenty-four elders sat on them. They were all clothed in white and had crowns on their heads.

From the throne came flashes of lightning and the rumble of thunder. And in front of the throne were seven torches with burning flames. This is the sevenfold Spirit of God. In front of the throne was a shiny sea of glass, sparkling like crystal. In the center and around the throne were four living beings, each covered with eyes, front and back.

All I can say is all Praise, Glory and Honor to you, forever and ever, Father.

Revelation 4:11 – You are worthy, O Lord our God to receive glory and honor and power. For you created all things, and they exist because you created what you pleased.

Revelation 5:11-12 – Then I looked again and I heard the voices of thousands and millions of angels around the throne and of the living beings and the elders. And they sang in a mighty chorus – Worthy is the Lamb who was slaughtered to receive power and riches and wisdom and strength and honor and glory and blessing.

Revelation 5:13 – And then I heard every creature in heaven and on earth and under the earth and in the sea. They sang – Blessing and honor and glory and power belong to the one sitting on the throne and to the Lamb forever and ever.

As I said before, so much happens in Revelation and during the end times that I do not want to say it or express it the wrong way. So please, read Revelation. Or get a book and read about Revelation. You will not be disappointed.

Revelation 19:11-16 – Then I saw heaven opened, and a white horse was standing there. Its rider was named Faithful and True, for he judges fairly and wages a righteous war. His eyes were like flames of fire, and on his head were many crowns. A name was written on them that no one understood except himself.

He wore a robe dipped in blood, and his title was the Word of God. The armies of heaven, dressed in the finest of pure white linen, followed him on white horses.

From his mouth came a sharp sword to strike down the nations. He will rule them with an iron rod. He will release the fierce wrath of God, the Almighty, like juice flowing from a winepress. On his robe at his thigh was written this title – King of all kings and Lord of all lords.

The devil and his evil minions (antichrist, and false prophet) do not win.

Revelation 19:20 – And the beast was captured, and with him the false prophet who did mighty miracles on behalf of the beast – miracles that deceived all who had accepted the mark of the beast and who worshipped his statue. Both the beast and his false prophet were thrown into the fiery lake of burning sulfur.

Revelation 20:1-3 –Then I saw an angel coming down from heaven with the key to the bottomless pit and a heavy chain in his hand. He seized the dragon – that old serpent, who is the devil and Satan – and bound him in chains for a thousand years. The angel threw him into the bottomless pit, which he then shut and locked so Satan could not deceive the nations anymore until the thousand years were finished. Afterward he must be released for a little while.

Revelation 20:7-8 – When the thousand years come to an end, Satan will be let out of his prison. He will go out to deceive the nations – called Gog and Magog – in every corner of the earth. He will gather them together for battle – a mighty army, as numberless as sand along the seashore.

Revelation 20:9 –And I saw them as they went up on the broad plain of the earth and surrounded God's people and the beloved city. But fire from heaven came down on the attacking armies and consumed them.

Revelation 20:10 – Then the devil, who had deceived them, was thrown into the fiery lake of burning sulfur, joining the beast and the false prophet. There they will be tormented day and night forever and ever.

A new heaven and a new earth.

Revelation 21:1-7 – Then I saw a new heaven and a new earth, for the old heaven and the old earth had disappeared.

And the sea was also gone. And I saw the holy city, the new Jerusalem, coming down from God out of heaven like a bride beautifully dressed for her husband.

I heard a loud shout from the throne, saying, Look God's home is now among his people! He will live with them and they will be his people. God himself will be with them. He will wipe every tear from their eyes, and there will be no more death or sorrow or crying or pain. All these things are gone forever.

And the one sitting on the throne said – Look I am making everything new! And then he said to me, write this down, for what I tell you is trustworthy and true.

And he also said - It is finished. I am the Alpha and the Omega – the Beginning and the End. To all who are thirsty I will give freely from the springs of the water of life. All who are victorious will inherit all these blessings, and I will be their God and they will be my children.

A new Jerusalem – wait until you read this….. WOW (which is mom upside down, by the way)

Revelation 21:14 – So he took me in the Spirit to a great, high mountain, and he showed me the holy city, Jerusalem, descending out of heaven from God. It shone with the glory of God and sparkled like a precious stone – like jasper as clear as crystal. The city wall was broad and high, with twelve gates guarded by twelve angels. And the names of the twelve tribes of Israel were written on the gates.

There were three gates on each side – east, north, south and west. The wall of the city had twelve foundation stones, and on them were written the names of the twelve apostles of the Lamb.

Revelation 21:18-21 – The wall was made of jasper, and the city was pure gold as clear as glass. The wall of the city was built on foundation stones inlaid with twelve precious stones: the first was jasper, the second sapphire, the third agate, the fourth emerald, the fifth onyx, the six carnelian, the seventh chrysolite, the eighth beryl, the ninth topaz, the tenth chrysoprase, the eleventh jacinth, the twelfth amethyst. The twelve gates were made of pearls – each gate from a single pearl. And the main street was pure gold, as clear as glass.

Revelation 21:2-27 – I saw no temple in the city, for the Lord God Almighty and the Lamb are its temple. And the city has no need of sun or moon, for the glory of God illuminates the city and the Lamb is its light. The nations will walk in its light and the kings of the world will enter the city in all its glory. Its gates will never be closed at the end of the day because there is no night there. And all the nations will bring their glory and honor into the city. Nothing evil will be allowed to enter, nor anyone who practices shameful idolatry and dishonesty – but only those whose names are written in the Lamb's Book of Life.

Revelation 22:1-6 – Then the angel showed me a river with the water of life, clear as crystal, flowing from the throne of God and of the Lamb.

It flowed down the center of the main street. On each side of the river grew a tree of live, bearing twelve crops of fruit, with a fresh crop each month. The leaves were used for medicine to heal the nations.

We will see His face.

No longer will there be a curse upon anything. For the throne of God and of the Lamb will be there and his servants will worship him. And they will see his face and his name will be written on their foreheads. And there will be no night there – no need for lamps or sun – for the Lord God will shine on them. And they will reign forever and ever.

Then the angel said to me – everything you have heard and seen is trustworthy and true. The Lord God, who inspires his prophets has sent his angel to tell his servants what will happen soon.

Revelation 22:7 – Look, I am coming soon! Blessed are those who obey the words of prophecy written in this book.

This is why I do not want to add or remove anything in the book of Revelation by mistake. I don't want to take any chances. Read the below verses.

Revelation 22:17-19 – The Spirit and the bride say – "Come". Let anyone who hears this say – "Come". Let anyone who is thirsty come. Let anyone who desires drink freely from the water of life.

And I solemnly declare to everyone who hears the words of prophecy written in this book: If anyone adds anything to what is written here, God will add to that person the plagues described in this book.

And if anyone removes any of the words from this book of prophecy, God will remove that person's share in the tree of life and in the holy city that are described in this book.

The last sentences of the Bible says it all -----

Revelation 20-21 – He who is the faithful witness to all these things says, Yes, I am coming soon!

Amen! Come, Lord Jesus!

May the Grace of the Lord Jesus be with God's holy people.

CHAPTER 12
The Devil Can't Have Me

Apollo

The Bible – A Verse A Day

In our busy lives, it can feel like a chore just to read the Bible. I can speak for me – after working a long, stress filled day, I am exhausted. The last thing I want to do is read the Bible. Give me something mindless – like a celebrity filled mind numbing magazine with pictures that I can just look at. But we really should take the time and read the Bible. Even if it is just one verse a night.

I have peppered some of my favorite Bible verses throughout this book. This is actually lazy on my part. I figured if I want to go back and read some inspirational Bible verses it might be a little quicker to find them. I hope this works for you too.

The Lord's Prayer

Always remember the prayer Jesus taught…

(Matthew 6:9-13, Luke 11:2-4)

> Our Father, Who Art in Heaven
> Hollowed Be Thy Name
> Thy Kingdom Come
> Thy Will Be Done On Earth As It Is In Heaven
> Give Us This Day Our Daily Bread
> And Forgive Us Our Trespasses
> As We Forgive Those Who Trespass Against Us
> And Lead Us Not Into Temptation
> Deliver Us From Evil
> Amen

I Hope I Meet You In Heaven

In closing this book, there are just a few things I would like to say…

No matter what happens in your life, no matter what trials you may face, no matter how dire the situation, remember to **ALWAYS FOCUS ON GOD**

Remember to start your day and end your day the same, and do this in between – all day – as much as possible **PRAY**

Love each other; forgive people that do wrong things to you or are mean; encourage each other to **NEVER GIVE UP ON GOD**

Read the Bible, every day if you can – even a verse a day. Keep growing in the Word of God. Give your problems to God and do not take them back. **TRUST GOD**

May God bless each of you and your family.

I hope to meet you in Heaven.

And remember what my mom said to me…… Repeat it often…..

The Devil Can't Have Me No Matter What, I'll Hit Him In The Head and I'll Kick Him In The Butt……

www.ingramcontent.com/pod-product-compliance
Lightning Source LLC
Chambersburg PA
CBHW040624240426
43666CB00020BA/2916